Ramen Noodle Soup And Thai Cookbook

2 Books In 1: Over 150 Recipes Cookbook For Classic Asian Comfort Food

By

Maki Blanc

RAMEN
COOKBOOK

70 Recipes for Preparing at Home Traditional Japanese Noodle Soup.

By

Maki Blanc

© **Copyright 2021 by Maki Blanc - All rights reserved.**

This document is geared towards providing exact and reliable information in regard to the topic and issue covered. The publication is sold with the idea that the publisher is not required to render accounting, officially permitted, or otherwise, qualified services. If advice is necessary, legal or professional, a practiced individual in the profession should be ordered.

From a Declaration of Principles which was accepted and approved equally by a Committee of the American Bar Association and a Committee of Publishers and Associations.

In no way is it legal to reproduce, duplicate, or transmit any part of this document in either electronic means or in printed format. Recording of this publication is strictly prohibited and any storage of this document is not allowed unless with written permission from the publisher. All rights reserved.

The information provided herein is stated to be truthful and consistent, in that any liability, in terms of inattention or otherwise, by any usage or abuse of any policies, processes, or directions contained within is the solitary and utter responsibility of the recipient reader. Under no circumstances will any legal responsibility or blame be held against the publisher for any reparation, damages, or monetary loss due to the information herein, either directly or indirectly.

Respective authors own all copyrights not held by the publisher.

The information herein is offered for informational purposes solely and is universal as so. The presentation of the information is without contract or any type of guarantee assurance.

The trademarks that are used are without any consent, and the publication of the trademark is without permission or backing by the trademark owner. All trademarks and brands within this book are for clarifying purposes only and are owned by the owners themselves, not affiliated with this document.

Contents

INTRODUCTION 12

CHAPTER 1: INTRODUCTION TO JAPANESE NOODLE SOUPS 14

1.1 History and Origin of Ramen 14

1.2 Ramen According to the Nutrition and Dietetics................ 16

1.3 Various Ingredients Used in Ramen..................................... 17

CHAPTER 2: THE WORLD OF RAMEN BREAKFAST RECIPES 20

2.1 Japanese Ramen Scrambled Eggs Recipe 21

2.2 Japanese Bacon and Egg Ramen Recipe 22

2.3 Japanese Ramen Omelet Recipe.. 24

2.4 Japanese Ramen with Soft Boiled Eggs Recipe 25

2.5 Japanese Miso Ramen with Boiled Eggs Recipe 27

2.6 Japanese Bacon, Egg and Cheese Breakfast Ramen Recipe 28

2.7 Japanese Ramen with Tofu and Eggs Recipe..................... 30

2.8 Japanese Chicken Ramen with Bok Choy and Soy Eggs Recipe 32

2.9 Japanese Egg Tonkotsu Ramen Recipe 33

2.10 Japanese Scallops and Egg Ramen Recipe........................ 34

CHAPTER 3: THE WORLD OF RAMEN LUNCH RECIPES 37

3.1 Japanese Ramen Noodle Soup Recipe 37

3.2 Japanese Duck Ramen Recipes 39

3.3 Japanese Sapporo Ramen Recipe 40

3.4 Japanese Miso Ramen Recipe 42

3.5 Japanese Shoyu Ramen Recipe 43

3.6 Japanese Tantanmen Ramen Recipe 45

3.7 Japanese Spicy Pork Ramen Recipe 46

3.8 Japanese Roast Pork Ramen Recipe 48

3.9 Japanese Chargrilled Chicken Ramen Recipe 49

3.10 Japanese Lemongrass, Chicken and Ginger Ramen Recipe 51

3.11 Japanese Spicy Beef Ramen Recipe 52

3.12 Japanese Prawn Ramen Recipe 54

3.13 Japanese Ramen Noodle Salad Recipe 56

3.14 Japanese Mongolian Beef Ramen Recipe 57

3.15 Japanese Meatball Ramen Recipe 59

3.16 Japanese Ramen Noodle Skillet with Steak Recipe 60

3.17 Japanese Cheese Ramen Recipe 62

3.18 Japanese Ramen Burger Recipe 64

3.19 Japanese Garlic and Shrimp Ramen Recipe 66

3.20 Japanese Beef and Ramen Stir-Fry Recipe 67

CHAPTER 4: THE WORLD OF RAMEN DINNER RECIPES 70

4.1 Japanese Parmesan and Garlic Ramen Recipe 70

4.2 Japanese Ginger and Beef Stir-Fry Ramen Recipe 72

4.3 Japanese Peanut and Chicken Ramen Recipe 73

4.4 Japanese Roasted Chicken Ramen Recipe 75

4.5 Japanese Sirarcha and Shrimp Ramen Recipe 77

4.6 Japanese Bacon Ramen Soup Recipe 79

4.7 Japanese Sweet and Sour Pork Ramen Recipe 81

4.8 Japanese Cheesy Tuna Ramen Recipe 82

4.9 Japanese Ramen and Tomato Soup Recipe 85

4.10 Japanese Chili Ramen Recipe 86

4.11 Japanese Chicken and Mushroom Ramen Recipe 88

4.12 Japanese Parmesan Chicken Ramen Recipe 89

4.13 Japanese Chicken Lo Mein Ramen Recipe 91

4.14 Japanese Shrimp Ramen Recipe 92

4.15 Japanese Green Pepper and Chicken Ramen Recipe 94

4.16 Japanese Creamy Tonkotsu Ramen Recipe 97

4.17 Japanese Miso and Crispy Pork Ramen Recipe 98

4.18 Japanese Shio and Pork Ramen Recipe 100

4.19 Japanese Ramen Noodle Coleslaw Recipe 102

4.20 Japanese Instant Ramen Noodle Recipe 103

CHAPTER 5: THE WORLD OF VEGETARIAN RAMEN RECIPES 104

5.1 Japanese Spicy Vegetarian Ramen Recipe 104

5.2 Japanese Shiitake Mushroom Ramen Recipe 105

5.3 Japanese Miso Vegetarian Ramen Noodle Soup Recipe 107

5.4 Japanese Teriyaki Tofu Ramen Recipe 109

5.5 Japanese Tonkotsu Vegetarian Ramen Recipe 110

5.6 Japanese Pantry Vegetarian Ramen Recipe 112

5.7 Japanese Marinated Tofu and Vegetable Ramen Recipe 113

5.8 Japanese Creamy Vegan Ramen Recipe 115

5.9 Japanese Creamy Sesame Ramen Broth Recipe 116

5.10 Japanese Spicy Broccoli Ramen Recipe 118

5.11 Japanese Cauliflower Ramen Recipe 119

5.12 Japanese Hot and Sour Dashi Ramen Recipe 121

5.13 Japanese Spicy Carrot Ramen Recipe 122

5.14 Japanese Vegan Shōyu Ramen with Potatoes Recipe 123

5.15 Japanese Ginger Ramen Recipe 126

5.16 Japanese Vegan Ramen Taco Recipe 127

5.17 Japanese Vegetarian Spicy Peanut Tempeh Ramen Recipe 128

5.18 Japanese Spicy Soy Milk Ramen Recipe 129

5.19 Japanese Vegetarian Ginger and Scallion Ramen Recipe 131

5.20 Japanese Crispy Sesame Tofu Ramen Recipe 132

CONCLUSION 134

INTRODUCTION 138

CHAPTER 1: INTRODUCTION TO THAI FOOD 139

1.1 History and Origin of Thai Food 139

1.2 History of Traditional Thai Dishes 140

1.3 Evolution of Thai Food over Time 141

1.4 Thai Foods According to Nutrition and Dietetics 141

1.5 Key Ingredients Used in Thai Food 142

CHAPTER 2: THE WORLD OF TRADITIONAL THAI BREAKFAST RECIPES 146

2.1 Salapao Recipe 146

2.2 Khao Neow Sang Kaya Recipe 147

2.3 Khanum Pang (Thai Waffles) Recipe 149

2.4 Khanom Recipe 150

2.5 Khai Luak (Thai Soft Eggs) Recipe 152

2.6 Khao Rad Gyang (Thai Breakfast Rice and Curry) Recipe 153

2.7 Khao Yum (Thai Breakfast Rice Salad) Recipe 155

2.8 Thai Breakfast Rice and Shrimp Soup Recipe 156

2.9 Thai Styled Traditional Omelet Recipe 158

2.10 Thai Breakfast Ginger and Rice Soup Recipe 159

2.11 Spicy Thai Breakfast Noodles Recipe 161

2.12 Thai Fried Eggs Recipe 162

CHAPTER 3: THE WORLD OF TRADITIONAL THAI LUNCH RECIPES 164

3.1 Thai Coconut and Noodle Soup Recipe **164**

3.2 Thai Curry Mud Crab Recipe **165**

3.3 Thai Chicken and Sweet Potato Soup Recipe **167**

3.4 Thai Pork and Peanut Curry Recipe **169**

3.5 Thai Beef Stir-Fry Recipe **170**

3.6 Thai Minced Chicken Salad Recipe **172**

3.7 Thai Lemongrass Beef Stew with Noodles Recipe **173**

3.8 Thai Butternut Squash Soup Recipe **175**

3.9 Thai Green Chicken Soup Recipe **176**

3.10 Thai Baked Chicken and Rice Recipe **178**

3.11 Thai Pork Belly with Basil and Tofu Recipe **179**

3.12 Thai Red Meatball Curry Recipe **181**

3.13 Thai Sesame Chicken Salad Recipe **182**

3.14 Spicy Thai Prawn Noodles Recipe **184**

3.15 Thai Red Salmon Curry Recipe **185**

CHAPTER 4: THE WORLD OF TRADITIONAL THAI DINNER RECIPES 187

4.1 Thai Peanut Chicken and Noodles Recipe **187**

4.2 Thai Red Curry Chicken and Vegetable Recipe **188**

4.3 Thai Noodles with Spicy Peanut Sauce Recipe **190**

4.4 Thai Coconut and Beef Curry Recipe **191**

4.5 Thai Coconut and Beef Salad Recipe..192

4.6 Thai Green Chicken Thighs Recipe..194

4.7 Thai Basil Pork Stir-Fry Recipe...195

4.8 Thai Green Chicken Curry with Vegetables Recipe....................197

4.9 Thai Mussels in Basil Coconut Sauce Recipe..............................198

4.10 Thai Pumpkin and Sweet Potato Curry Recipe........................200

4.11 Thai Tofu Fried Rice Recipe..201

4.12 Thai Chicken Pad Thai Recipe..203

4.13 Thai Sour and Spicy Soup Recipe..204

4.14 Thai Pumpkin and Coconut Curry Recipe................................205

4.15 Thai Grilled Salmon Recipe...207

4.16 Thai Red Beef Curry Recipe..208

4.17 Thai Coconut Curry Recipe...210

4.18 Thai Pumpkin and Vegetable Soup Recipe...............................211

CHAPTER 5: THE WORLD OF TRADITIONAL THAI DESSERT RECIPES..213

5.1 Thai Coconut Pudding Recipe..213

5.2 Thai Fruit Salad Recipe...214

5.3 Thai Mung Bean Pudding Recipe..216

5.4 Thai Mango Sticky Rice Recipe..217

5.5 Thai Mango Tapioca Pudding Recipe...219

5.6 Thai Fried Bananas Recipe...220

5.7 Thai Steamed Banana Cake Recipe 221

5.8 Thai Tea Cake Recipe 222

5.9 Thai Banana Spring Rolls Recipe 224

5.10 Thai Mango Cake Recipe 224

5.11 Thai Coconut Cake Recipe 227

5.12 Thai Mango Ice Cream Recipe 228

5.13 Thai Sticky Black Rice Pudding Recipe 229

5.14 Thai Egg and Coconut Custard Recipe 231

5.15 Thai Sweet Corn Pudding Recipe 232

CHAPTER 6: THE WORLD OF TRADITIONAL THAI RECIPES EATEN ONLY BY THAI PEOPLE 234

6.1 Patonga (Thai Breakfast Donut) Recipe 234

6.2 Khanom Kharuk (Thai Mini Pancakes) Recipe 235

6.3 Jauk (The Rice Porridge) Recipe 236

6.4 Khao Tom (The Rice Porridge Soup) Recipe 238

6.5 Dim Sum (Thai Steamed Buns) Recipe 240

6.6 Thai Sweet Rice Cakes Recipe 242

6.7 Thai Steamed Pandan Cakes Recipe 243

6.8 Thai Carrot and Radish Salad Recipe 245

6.9 Thai Fish Broth with Vegetables Recipe 246

6.10 Thai Prawn and Coconut Soup Recipe 248

CONCLUSION 250

Introduction

Ramen are the most famous noodle dishes in Japan. These boiled noodles are essentially served in various flavorful soups with numerous toppings. Chukamen noodles which are for the most part made with wheat flour and kansui are used for ramen dishes. There are numerous types of ramen flavors in Japan. They are used in different flavors of soups, garnishes, broth, noodle texture in ramens, and this is only the tip of an iceberg. Making a tasty ramen is not very simple if you are preparing it from scratch.

The flavor of ramen predominantly relies upon the soup. Ramen cooks generally train themselves for quite a while to be able to make great ramen soup. Each ramen shop has its own particular manner to make ramen soup. So, there are countless ways to make ramen soup. Chicken bone, pork bone, dried sardines, as well as kombu are utilized to make soup stock for ramen.

You can prepare Japanese ramen soup at home by learning the list of various ingredients that you will need to start cooking. By reading this wonderful book, you will get the detailed knowledge regarding the nutritional value and history of ramen. This book contains over 70 different breakfast, lunch, dinner, and vegetarian ramen recipes. You can easily start cooking at home with the detailed instructions present below each recipe. So start reading and start cooking today!

Chapter 1: Introduction to Japanese Noodle Soups

Ramen is a noodle soup dish that was initially imported from China and has become perhaps the most mainstream dishes in Japan for the past many years. Ramen are cheap and broadly accessible. These two factors additionally make them an ideal choice for tourists. Ramen cafés can be found in each corner of the country. These cafes produce incalculable varieties of this basic noodle dish.

Typical Ramen noodles are long and flexible. However, innumerable assortments of ramen exist that vary from slender to thick and wavy. Some ramen cafes permit you to modify your noodle soup in many ways, for example, by permitting you to choose its thickness (slight, ordinary or thick) or doneness (normal or firm).

1.1 History and Origin of Ramen

The ramen noodle has extended its compass across numerous lands and nations framing profound roots in many of these societies. Actually, the noodle has effectively managed to form connections with Japan's lifestyle and history as well. Ramen has a long history in Japan, changing as the conditions of the nation changed too.

The origin of the first ramen is obscure. Yet, a legend says that ramen came from a dish acquired from China. The principal legend sets up Shu Shunsui, a researcher from China, as the person who brought the ramen formula to Japan.

Shu Shunsui was a Chinese exile of the Ming government who came to fill in as a consultant to the Japanese primitive master Tokugawa Mitsukuni. Verifiable records show that Shu Shunsui advised Mitsukini on what to add to his udon soup to make it taste better. This dish is supposed to be the first ramen that was eaten in Japan. While the facts confirm that Chinese culture vigorously affected Japanese culture at that time. Yet, an authentic record of Mitsukini cooking ramen does not exist.

Another legend interfaces the origin of ramen. It happened when Japan opened its ports to the rest of the world. Japan's ports pulled in Chinese voyagers, and a Chinese noodle soup called laa-mein was brought into Japan. This dish fills in as a possible archetype to the ramen today even though laa-mein did not have any garnishes and was not like the advanced ramen.

The last and most conceivable hypothesis relates the source of the ramen to a shop called Rai Ken in Tokyo during the 1900s. Rai Ken utilized Chinese laborers and served a noodle dish called Shina Soba. Shina Soba had added fixings that looked like todays ramen. These fixings include cooked pork, Japanese fish cake, and nori sheets into one dish. Japan was getting industrialized and more urbanized during this time-frame. Japan's industrialization and urbanization helped in promoting ramen. Shina soba was a modest and filling dish, giving a lot of calories to Japanese metropolitan laborers.

Today ramen has become an image and chronicled figure of Japanese culture and history. Ramen has broadened its span universally all throughout the planet.

Conventional ramen is extremely necessary in Japanese culture. In any case, it is still difficult to get credible Japanese ramen except if one is close to the huge assorted urban communities. Now, ramen can be found at practically any general store. Despite the fact that ramen has now become a worldwide pattern, its profound roots will consistently be appended to Japan's set of experiences.

1.2 Ramen According to the Nutrition and Dietetics

The conventional Japanese eating routine is full of healthy food sources. It has all the basic macronutrients that are essential for a healthy and nutritious diet. Japanese traditional cuisine depends on conventional Japanese cooking, otherwise called "washoku." This cooking comprises of adding fresh and healthy ingredients into the dishes to make sure the health of the individuals is not compromised. This eating design is rich in supplements and may give various medical advantages. These advantages may include improved weight reduction, digestion and absorption, long life span, and overall health.

Ramen noodles are the healthiest when joined with different fixings to make a nutritious feast. Ramen is incredible to use as a base for a variety of healthy dishes and it is not difficult to prepare on your own. Ramen noodles are healthy as they contain protein and carbohydrates in good amounts. Fats are present in a very low quantity that is almost negligible.

You can also add vegetables in your bowl of ramen. This will add to a generous flavor and add supplements to the supper. Carrots, spinach, broccoli, zucchini, cauliflower and peppers will not just give you extraordinary taste, they will give you a decent serving of vitamins, minerals and fiber in each bite. Try adding various blends of vegetables with various ramen flavors to discover the combination that you like the best. Ramen bowls consistently go extraordinary with fresh chicken, beef meat, fish or pork for the protein your body needs.

Investigate the possibilities and look at how easy it is to change a generally extraordinary tasting and healthy bowl of ramen noodles into an even healthier feast in minutes by adding different ingredients into it.

1.3 Various Ingredients Used in Ramen

Following are the different ingredients that are used in making ramen noodles at home:

1. Stocks

Stocks are generally from pork or chicken bones or a combination of the two. Dashi stock is made utilizing bonito chips which is a dried fish. Rather than making your own stock, you can purchase instant dashi stock sachets.

2. Mirin

Mirin is a Japanese sweet rice wine, which is currently broadly accessible in the global food walkways of most of the stores. It has a sweet surface and adds pleasant flavor to a dish.

3. Sake

Japanese sake is utilized in numerous Japanese dishes. However, you can use a substitute Chinese Shaoxing rice wine, which is more broadly accessible. Shaoxing rice wine adds another layer when utilizing delicate flavors in Japanese and Chinese cooking and is fabulous for adding flavor to meat when cooking and in marinades.

4. Nori sheets

Nori sheets are very healthy and usually used in different ramen dishes. They add protein into the ramen. They have an incredible flavor and are loved by many people around the world.

5. Kimchi

This is a Korean derived dish. It is fermented cabbage that is used in ramen noodles as a side dish. Kimchi adds a salty and tangy flavor into the ramen noodles.

6. Japanese curry sauce

These curry sauce packets contain a bar of curry concentrate, which can be broken off in pieces and added to stock bases for a curried broth. The flavor is similar to a Chinese curry paste and makes a great delicately flavored curry broth. It is commonly used in ramen noodles.

7. Soy sauce

It is the most common sauce all around the world. It is added to ramen noodles and imparts a unique taste to the noodles. Soy sauce comes in two varieties i.e. light soy sauce and dark soy sauce.

Chapter 2: The World of Ramen Breakfast Recipes

Having Ramen for breakfast is customary in two districts of Japan, and many nearby ramen shops carry on this tradition. These districts are Fukushima and Kitakata. All the breakfast dishes mentioned below are healthy and are traditionally eaten in these districts of Japan:

Basic Instructions to Cook Ramen:

- Take a large saucepan.
- Add water into the saucepan.
- Boil the water.
- Add the ramen noodles when the water reaches the boiling temperature.
- Cook the ramen for seven minutes approximately.
- Make sure not to overcook the ramen noodles.
- Drain the noodles and add a teaspoon of oil into the ramen.
- The oil will prevent the ramen from sticking.
- You can use this method of boiling the ramen in all of the recipes below.

2.1 Japanese Ramen Scrambled Eggs Recipe

Preparation Time: 30 minutes
Cooking Time: 10 minutes
Serving: 4

Ingredients:

- Chopped chives, one teaspoon
- Butter, two tablespoon
- Cooked chickpeas, half cup
- Tofu cubes, half pound
- Salt, to taste
- Black pepper, to taste
- Tamari paste, two teaspoon
- Eggs, four
- Mirin paste, one tablespoon
- Chopped garlic, one teaspoon
- Ramen noodles, four packs

Instructions:
1. Take a large pan.
2. Add the butter and let it meltdown.
3. Add in the eggs.
4. Add in the tamari paste.

5. Mix the tamari paste and eggs.
6. Add the chopped garlic.
7. Scramble the mixture.
8. Add in the salt and pepper.
9. Add in the chickpeas and rest of the ingredients in the end.
10. Boil the ramen noodles according to the instructions on the pack.
11. Drain the noodles and add them into the pan.
12. Mix all the ingredients well and then dish them out.
13. Garnish the fresh chopped chives on top.
14. Your dish is ready to be served.

2.2 Japanese Bacon and Egg Ramen Recipe

Preparation Time: 30 minutes
Cooking Time: 10 minutes
Serving: 4

Ingredients:

- Chopped chives, one teaspoon
- Butter, two tablespoon
- Chopped bacon, half pound
- Salt, to taste

- Black pepper, to taste
- Tamari paste, two teaspoon
- Eggs, four
- Mirin paste, one tablespoon
- Chopped garlic, one teaspoon
- Ramen noodles, four packs

Instructions:

1. Take a large pan.
2. Add the butter and let it meltdown.
3. Add in the chopped bacons.
4. Add in the tamari paste.
5. Mix all the ingredients well.
6. Add the chopped garlic.
7. Add in the rest of the ingredients in the end.
8. Scramble the mixture.
9. Add in the salt and pepper.
10. Boil the ramen noodles according to the instructions on the pack.
11. Drain the noodles and add them into the pan.
12. Mix all the ingredients well and then dish them out.
13. Garnish the fresh chopped chives on top.
14. Your dish is ready to be served.

2.3 Japanese Ramen Omelet Recipe

Preparation Time: 30 minutes
Cooking Time: 10 minutes
Serving: 4

Ingredients:

- Onions, half cup
- Rice wine, one tablespoon
- Eggs, four
- Black pepper, to taste
- Salt, to taste
- Starch, a quarter teaspoon
- Ramen noodles, four packs
- Ginger, one slice
- Soy sauce, one tablespoon
- Oil, one tablespoon
- Cilantro, as required

Instructions:
1. Take a large bowl.
2. Add all the ingredients into the bowl.

3. Make the egg mixture.
4. Take a large pan.
5. Heat a pan and then add the oil into the pan.
6. Add the egg mixture on top when the oil heats up.
7. Let the eggs cook from the bottom.
8. Now slowly start to flip the egg.
9. Dish out the egg when both the sides turn golden brown.
10. Garnish the eggs by adding chopped cilantro on top.
11. Your dish is ready to be served.

2.4 Japanese Ramen with Soft Boiled Eggs Recipe

Preparation Time: 30 minutes
Cooking Time: 10 minutes
Serving: 4

Ingredients:

- Chopped chives, one teaspoon
- Butter, two tablespoon
- Salt, to taste
- Black pepper, to taste
- Tamari paste, two teaspoon
- Eggs, four

- Mirin paste, one tablespoon
- Chopped garlic, one teaspoon
- Ramen noodles, four packs

Instructions:

1. Boil the eggs.
2. Make sure to boil the eggs for five minutes only.
3. Take a large pan.
4. Add the butter and let it meltdown.
5. Add in the tamari paste.
6. Mix all the ingredients well.
7. Add the chopped garlic.
8. Add in the rest of the ingredients in the end.
9. Scramble the mixture.
10. Add in the salt and pepper.
11. Boil the ramen noodles according to the instructions on the pack.
12. Drain the noodles and add them into the pan.
13. Mix all the ingredients well and then dish them out.
14. Peel the eggs and place it on the ramen.
15. Garnish the fresh chopped chives on top.
16. Your dish is ready to be served.

2.5 Japanese Miso Ramen with Boiled Eggs Recipe

Preparation Time: 30 minutes
Cooking Time: 10 minutes
Serving: 4

Ingredients:

- Chopped chives, one teaspoon
- Butter, two tablespoon
- Salt, to taste
- Black pepper, to taste
- Miso paste, two teaspoon
- Eggs, four
- Mirin paste, one tablespoon
- Chopped garlic, one teaspoon
- Ramen noodles, four packs

Instructions:
1. Boil the eggs.
2. Make sure to boil the eggs for ten minutes only.

3. Take a large pan.
4. Add the butter and let it meltdown.
5. Add in the miso paste.
6. Mix all the ingredients well.
7. Add the chopped garlic.
8. Add in the rest of the ingredients in the end.
9. Scramble the mixture.
10. Add in the salt and pepper.
11. Boil the ramen noodles according to the instructions on the pack.
12. Drain the noodles and add them into the pan.
13. Mix all the ingredients well and then dish them out.
14. Peel the eggs and place them on the ramen.
15. Garnish the fresh chopped chives on top.
16. Your dish is ready to be served.

2.6 Japanese Bacon, Egg and Cheese Breakfast Ramen Recipe

Preparation Time: 30 minutes

Cooking Time: 10 minutes

Serving: 4

Ingredients:

- Chopped chives, one teaspoon
- Butter, two tablespoon
- Chopped bacon, half pound
- Salt, to taste
- Black pepper, to taste
- Cheese, one cup
- Eggs, four
- Mirin paste, one tablespoon
- Chopped garlic, one teaspoon
- Ramen noodles, four packs

Instructions:

1. Take a large pan.
2. Add the butter and let it meltdown.
3. Add in the chopped bacons.
4. Mix all the ingredients well.
5. Add the chopped garlic.
6. Add in the rest of the ingredients in the end.
7. Scramble the mixture.
8. Add in the salt and pepper.
9. Boil the ramen noodles according to the instructions on the pack.

10. Drain the noodles and add them into the pan.
11. Mix all the ingredients well and then dish them out.
12. Your dish is ready to be served.

2.7 Japanese Ramen with Tofu and Eggs Recipe

Preparation Time: 30 minutes

Cooking Time: 10 minutes

Serving: 4

Ingredients:

- Chopped chives, one teaspoon
- Butter, two tablespoon
- Tofu cubes, half pound
- Salt, to taste
- Black pepper, to taste
- Tamari paste, as required
- Eggs, four
- Mirin paste, one tablespoon
- Chopped garlic, one teaspoon

Instructions:

1. Take a large pan.
2. Add the butter and let it meltdown.
3. Add in the eggs.
4. Add in the tamari paste.
5. Mix the tamari paste and eggs and then add the chopped garlic.
6. Scramble the mixture.
7. Add in the salt and pepper.
8. Add in the tofu cubes and rest of the ingredients in the end.
9. When the eggs are done, dish them out.
10. Add the fresh chopped chives on top.
11. Your dish is ready to be served.

2.8 Japanese Chicken Ramen with Bok Choy and Soy Eggs Recipe

Preparation Time: 30 minutes

Cooking Time: 10 minutes

Serving: 4

Ingredients:

- Onions, half cup
- Rice wine, one tablespoon
- Eggs, four
- Black pepper, to taste
- Salt, to taste
- Cooked chicken, one cup
- Ramen noodles, four packs
- Ginger, one teaspoon
- Bok choy, one cup
- Soy sauce, half cup
- Oil, one tablespoon
- Cilantro, as required

Instructions:
1. Take a large bowl.
2. Add all the ingredients into the bowl.
3. Make the egg mixture.
4. Take a large pan.
5. Heat a pan and then add the oil into the pan.
6. Add the egg mixture on top when the oil heats up.
7. Let the eggs cook from the bottom.
8. Scramble the eggs for ten minutes.
9. Garnish the eggs by adding chopped cilantro on top.
10. Your dish is ready to be served.

2.9 Japanese Egg Tonkotsu Ramen Recipe

Preparation Time: 30 minutes
Cooking Time: 10 minutes
Serving: 4

Ingredients:

- Chopped chives, one teaspoon
- Butter, two tablespoon
- Tonkatsu broth, one cup
- Salt, to taste
- Black pepper, to taste

- Tamari paste, two teaspoon
- Eggs, four
- Mirin paste, one tablespoon
- Chopped garlic, one teaspoon
- Ramen noodles, four packs

Instructions:
1. Take a large pan.
2. Add the butter and let it meltdown.
3. Add in the eggs.
4. Add in the tamari paste.
5. Mix the tamari paste and eggs.
6. Add the chopped garlic.
7. Scramble the mixture.
8. Add in the salt and pepper.
9. Add in the tonkatsu broth and rest of the ingredients in the end.
10. Mix all the ingredients well and then dish them out.
11. Garnish the fresh chopped chives on top.
12. Your dish is ready to be served.

2.10 Japanese Scallops and Egg Ramen Recipe

Preparation Time: 30 minutes

Cooking Time: 10 minutes
Serving: 4

Ingredients:

- Chopped cilantro, one teaspoon
- Butter, two tablespoon
- Chopped scallions, two cups
- Salt, to taste
- Black pepper, to taste
- Tamari paste, two teaspoon
- Eggs, four
- Mirin paste, one tablespoon
- Chopped garlic, one teaspoon
- Ramen noodles, four packs

Instructions:
1. Take a large pan.
2. Add the butter and let it meltdown.
3. Add in the chopped scallions.
4. Add in the tamari paste.
5. Mix all the ingredients well.
6. Add the chopped garlic.
7. Add in the rest of the ingredients in the end.
8. Scramble the mixture.

9. Add in the salt and pepper.
10. Boil the ramen noodles according to the instructions on the pack.
11. Drain the noodles and add them into the pan.
12. Mix all the ingredients well and then dish them out.
13. Garnish the fresh chopped cilantro on top.
14. Your dish is ready to be served.

Chapter 3: The World of Ramen Lunch Recipes

Japanese ramen lunch recipes are full of flavors. There are many varieties of ramen noodles that can be eaten during the lunch time. Following are some easy to make recipes that you can cook today:

3.1 Japanese Ramen Noodle Soup Recipe

Preparation Time: 20 minutes
Cooking Time: 20 minutes
Serving: 4

Ingredients:

- Ramen noodles, two packs
- Miso paste, one teaspoon
- Onion, one cup
- Bell peppers, one cup
- Japanese fresh herbs, half teaspoon
- Water, one cup
- Minced garlic, two tablespoon
- Minced ginger, two tablespoon
- Cilantro, half cup
- Diced carrots, one cup

- Olive oil, two tablespoon
- Water, half cup
- Vegetable stock, two cups
- Chopped tomatoes, one cup

Instructions:

1. Take a pan.
2. Add in the oil and onions.
3. Cook the onions until they become soft and fragrant.
4. Add in the chopped garlic and ginger.
5. Cook the mixture and add the tomatoes into it.
6. Add the spices.
7. Add the miso paste into it when the tomatoes are done.
8. Mix the ingredients carefully and cover the pan.
9. Add the vegetables and rest of the ingredients except the noodles.
10. Let the mixture boil.
11. Add the ramen noodles into the soup mixture.
12. Let the soup cook for ten to fifteen minutes straight.
13. Add cilantro on top.
14. Your dish is ready to be served.

3.2 Japanese Duck Ramen Recipes

Preparation Time: 30 minutes

Cooking Time: 10 minutes

Serving: 4

Ingredients:

- Tomato paste, one cup
- Sliced green onions, half cup
- Mirin paste, one teaspoon
- Cilantro, one cup
- Fresh ginger, one teaspoon
- Miso paste, one tablespoon
- Cooked and shredded duck meat, one cup
- Soy sauce, one tablespoon
- Japanese fresh herbs, half teaspoon
- Fresh shiso leaves, two tablespoon
- Fresh cilantro leaves, half cup
- Chopped tomatoes, half cup
- Ramen, as required

Instructions:

1. Add all the ingredients of the sauce i.e. miso paste, soy sauce, mirin paste and Japanese fresh herbs into a large pan.

2. Add the shredded duck meat, tomato paste, chopped tomatoes and the rest of the ingredients into the mixture.
3. Cook the dish for ten minutes.
4. Add the ramen into the mixture once the sauce is ready.
5. Mix the ramen well.
6. Cook the dish for five minutes.
7. Add the cilantro and the green onions into the dish.
8. Your dish is ready to be served.

3.3 Japanese Sapporo Ramen Recipe

Preparation Time: 30 minutes

Cooking Time: 10 minutes

Serving: 4

Ingredients:

- Bean sprouts, one cup
- Sliced green onions, half cup
- Mirin paste, one teaspoon
- Cilantro, one cup
- Bamboo shoots, one teaspoon
- Miso paste, one tablespoon
- Chashu pork meat, one cup

- Soy sauce, one tablespoon
- Cooking oil, two tablespoon
- Chopped garlic, one teaspoon
- Japanese fresh herbs, half teaspoon
- Fresh shiso leaves, two tablespoon
- Fresh cilantro leaves, half cup
- Dried chili flakes, two teaspoon
- Soft boiled eggs, four
- Ramen, as required

Instructions:
1. Take a large pan.
2. Add the cooking oil and chopped garlic into the pan.
3. Add Chashu pork meat into the pan.
4. Add all the spices into the mixture.
5. Cook the ingredients for five minutes.
6. Add the bean sprouts and ramen into the mixture.
7. Cook all the ingredients well.
8. Peel the soft boiled eggs and add them into the mixture.
9. Cook for five minutes.
10. Garnish the dish with cilantro and green onions.
11. Your dish is ready to be served.

3.4 Japanese Miso Ramen Recipe

Preparation Time: 20 minutes
Cooking Time: 10 minutes
Serving: 4

Ingredients:

- Miso paste, half cup
- Sliced green onions, half cup
- Mirin paste, one teaspoon
- Cilantro, one cup
- Fresh ginger, one teaspoon
- Soy sauce, one tablespoon
- Japanese fresh herbs, half teaspoon
- Fresh shiso leaves, two tablespoon
- Fresh cilantro leaves, half cup
- Minced lemon grass, one teaspoon
- Ramen, as required

Instructions:
1. Heat a large pan.
2. Add the miso paste and the rest of the ingredients into the mixture.
3. Cook the ingredients for ten minutes.

4. Add the ramen into the mixture once the sauce is ready.
5. Mix the ramen well.
6. Cook the dish for five minutes.
7. Add the cilantro into the dish.
8. Your dish is ready to be served.

3.5 Japanese Shoyu Ramen Recipe

Preparation Time: 20 minutes
Cooking Time: 20 minutes
Serving: 4

Ingredients:

- Ramen noodles, two packs
- Spicy chili bean sauce, two teaspoon
- Onion, one cup
- Dashi stock, two cups
- Japanese fresh herbs, half teaspoon
- Water, one cup
- Minced garlic, two tablespoon
- Minced ginger, two tablespoon
- Cilantro, half cup
- Fish cakes, one cup
- Chili oil, two tablespoon

- Shredded nori sheets, half cup
- Sheragi negi, two cups
- Chopped tomatoes, one cup

Instructions:
1. Take a pan.
2. Add in the oil and onions.
3. Cook the onions until they become soft and fragrant.
4. Add in the chopped garlic and ginger.
5. Cook the mixture for a few seconds.
6. Add the spices.
7. Add the sheragi negi into it when the spices are done.
8. Mix the ingredients carefully and cover the pan.
9. Add the fish cakes and rest of the ingredients except the noodles.
10. Let the mixture boil.
11. Add the ramen noodles into the soup mixture.
12. Let the soup cook for ten to fifteen minutes straight.
13. Add shredded nori sheets on top.
14. Your dish is ready to be served.

3.6 Japanese Tantanmen Ramen Recipe

Preparation Time: 30 minutes

Cooking Time: 10 minutes

Serving: 4

Ingredients:

- Minced pork, one cup
- Sliced green onions, half cup
- Tahini paste, one teaspoon
- Cilantro, one cup
- Fresh ginger, one teaspoon
- Oyster sauce, one tablespoon
- Rice wine, three tablespoon
- Soy sauce, one tablespoon
- Japanese fresh herbs, half teaspoon
- Chili oil, two tablespoon
- Fresh cilantro leaves, half cup
- Chopped tomatoes, half cup
- Ramen, as required
- Sesame seeds, half cup
- Bean sprouts, one cup
- Bok choy, one cup

Instructions:

1. Add all the ingredients of the sauce i.e. oyster sauce, soy sauce, rice wine and Japanese fresh herbs into a large pan.
2. Add the vegetables, minced pork, chopped tomatoes and the rest of the ingredients into the mixture.
3. Cook the dish for ten minutes.
4. Add the ramen into the mixture once the sauce is ready.
5. Mix the ramen well.
6. Cook the dish for five minutes.
7. Add the cilantro and the green onions into the dish.
8. Your dish is ready to be served.

3.7 Japanese Spicy Pork Ramen Recipe

Preparation Time: 30 minutes
Cooking Time: 10 minutes
Serving: 4

Ingredients:

- Chili paste, two tablespoon
- Sliced green onions, half cup
- Mirin paste, one teaspoon

- Fresh ginger, one teaspoon
- Miso paste, one tablespoon
- Cooked and shredded pork meat, one cup
- Soy sauce, one tablespoon
- Japanese fresh herbs, half teaspoon
- Fresh shiso leaves, two tablespoon
- Fresh cilantro leaves, half cup
- Chopped tomatoes, half cup
- Ramen, as required

Instructions:
1. Add all the ingredients of the sauce i.e. miso paste, soy sauce, mirin paste and Japanese fresh herbs into a large pan.
2. Add the shredded pork meat, chili paste, chopped tomatoes and the rest of the ingredients into the mixture.
3. Cook the dish for ten minutes.
4. Add the ramen into the mixture once the sauce is ready.
5. Mix the ramen well.
6. Cook the dish for five minutes.
7. Add the green onions into the dish.
8. Your dish is ready to be served.

3.8 Japanese Roast Pork Ramen Recipe

Preparation Time: 30 minutes
Cooking Time: 10 minutes
Serving: 4

Ingredients:

- Shredded nori sheets, two tablespoon
- Sliced green onions, half cup
- Mirin paste, one teaspoon
- Miso paste, one tablespoon
- Roasted and shredded pork meat, one cup
- Soy sauce, one tablespoon
- Japanese fresh herbs, half teaspoon
- Fresh shiso leaves, two tablespoon
- Fresh cilantro leaves, half cup
- Ramen, as required

Instructions:

1. Add all the ingredients of the sauce i.e. miso paste, soy sauce, mirin paste and Japanese fresh herbs into a large pan.
2. Add the roasted pork meat, shiso leaves, chopped tomatoes and the rest of the ingredients into the mixture.

3. Cook the dish for ten minutes.
4. Add the ramen into the mixture once the sauce is ready.
5. Mix the ramen well.
6. Cook the dish for five minutes.
7. Add the shredded nori sheets into the dish.
8. Your dish is ready to be served.

3.9 Japanese Chargrilled Chicken Ramen Recipe

Preparation Time: 30 minutes
Cooking Time: 20 minutes
Serving: 4

Ingredients:

- Chicken stock, two cups
- Crushed garlic, two
- Chicken pieces, one pound
- Salt, to taste
- Black pepper, to taste
- Olive oil, two tablespoon
- Dried white wine, one cup
- Onion, one cup
- All-purpose flour, three tablespoon
- Worcestershire sauce, two

- tablespoon
- Softened butter, three tablespoon
- Bay leaf, one
- Fresh thyme, two tablespoon
- Grated or sliced cheese, one cup
- Chopped cilantro, one cup
- Ramen noodles, four packs

Instructions:

1. Take a large skillet.
2. Add the oil and onions into the skillet.
3. Cook the onions until they turn golden brown.
4. Add the crushed garlic into the skillet.
5. Add the spices into the mixture.
6. Add all-purpose flour, Worcestershire sauce and dried white wine.
7. Add the butter and then add the chicken stock and ramen noodles.
8. Grill the chicken pieces over a grill pan.
9. Cut the chicken into long pieces.
10. Add the chicken into the ramen mixture.
11. The dish is ready to be served.

3.10 Japanese Lemongrass, Chicken and Ginger Ramen Recipe

Preparation Time: 30 minutes
Cooking Time: 10 minutes
Serving: 4

Ingredients:

- Tomato paste, one cup
- Sliced green onions, half cup
- Mirin paste, one teaspoon
- Cilantro, one cup
- Dried lemongrass, two teaspoon
- Fresh ginger slices, half cup
- Miso paste, one tablespoon
- Cooked and shredded chicken meat, one cup
- Soy sauce, one tablespoon
- Japanese fresh herbs, half teaspoon
- Fresh shiso leaves, two tablespoon
- Lemon juice, half cup
- Fresh cilantro leaves, half cup
- Chopped tomatoes, half cup
- Ramen, as required

Instructions:

1. Add all the ingredients of the sauce i.e. miso paste, soy sauce, mirin paste and Japanese fresh herbs into a large pan.
2. Add the shredded chicken meat, lemongrass, ginger slices, tomato paste, chopped tomatoes and the rest of the ingredients into the mixture.
3. Cook the dish for ten minutes.
4. Add the ramen into the mixture once the sauce is ready.
5. Mix the ramen well.
6. Cook the dish for five minutes.
7. Add the cilantro and the green onions into the dish.
8. Your dish is ready to be served.

3.11 Japanese Spicy Beef Ramen Recipe

Preparation Time: 30 minutes

Cooking Time: 10 minutes

Serving: 4

Ingredients:

- Chili paste, two tablespoon
- Sliced green onions, half cup
- Mirin paste, one teaspoon

- Fresh ginger, one teaspoon
- Miso paste, one tablespoon
- Cooked and shredded beef meat, one cup
- Soy sauce, one tablespoon
- Chopped garlic, one teaspoon
- Japanese fresh herbs, half teaspoon
- Fresh shiso leaves, two tablespoon
- Fresh cilantro leaves, half cup
- Chopped tomatoes, half cup
- Ramen, as required

Instructions:

1. Add all the ingredients of the sauce i.e. miso paste, soy sauce, mirin paste and Japanese fresh herbs into a large pan.
2. Add the shredded beef meat, chili paste, chopped tomatoes and the rest of the ingredients into the mixture.
3. Cook the dish for ten minutes.
4. Add the ramen into the mixture once the sauce is ready.
5. Mix the ramen well.
6. Cook the dish for five minutes.
7. Add the green onions into the dish.
8. Your dish is ready to be served.

3.12 Japanese Prawn Ramen Recipe

Preparation Time: 20 minutes
Cooking Time: 20 minutes
Serving: 4

Ingredients:

- Ramen noodles, two packs
- Miso paste, one teaspoon
- Onion, one cup
- Prawns, one pound
- Bell peppers, one cup
- Japanese fresh herbs, half teaspoon
- Water, one cup
- Minced garlic, two tablespoon
- Minced ginger, two tablespoon
- Cilantro, half cup
- Diced carrots, one cup
- Olive oil, two tablespoon
- Water, half cup
- Vegetable stock, two cups
- Chopped tomatoes, one cup

Instructions:
1. Take a pan.
2. Add in the oil and onions.
3. Cook the onions until they become soft and fragrant.
4. Add in the chopped garlic and ginger.
5. Cook the mixture and add the tomatoes into it.
6. Add the spices.
7. Add the miso paste into it when the tomatoes are done.
8. Mix the ingredients carefully and cover the pan.
9. Add the prawns, vegetables and rest of the ingredients except the noodles.
10. Let the mixture boil.
11. Add the ramen noodles into the soup mixture.
12. Let the soup cook for ten to fifteen minutes straight.
13. Add cilantro on top.
14. Your dish is ready to be served.

3.13 Japanese Ramen Noodle Salad Recipe

Preparation Time: 20 minutes
Cooking Time: 40 minutes
Serving: 2

Ingredients:
- Ginger powder, one tablespoon
- Chicken shredded, two cups
- Garlic powder, two teaspoon
- Maple syrup, half teaspoon
- Sesame oil, one teaspoon
- Soy sauce, one teaspoon
- Sriracha, one tablespoon
- Lime juice, one tablespoon
- Salt, to taste
- Ramen noodles, four packs
- Pepper, to taste

Instructions:
1. Boil the ramen noodles in a large pot full of water.
2. Drain the noodles when they are cooked.
3. Take a large bowl and add boiled noodles into it.
4. Add the ginger and garlic powder.
5. Mix well so that everything mixes well.

6. Add lime juice, maple syrup, cooked shredded chicken, Japanese red chili and soy sauce.
7. Add the salt and pepper as you like.
8. Add the sesame oil and mix well so that a homogeneous mixture is obtained.
9. Add the sriracha into the mixture.
10. Mix everything well.
11. The salad is ready to be served.

3.14 Japanese Mongolian Beef Ramen Recipe

Preparation Time: 30 minutes
Cooking Time: 10 minutes
Serving: 4

Ingredients:

- Nori paste, two tablespoon
- Sliced green onions, half cup
- Mirin paste, one teaspoon
- Fresh ginger, one teaspoon
- Miso paste, one tablespoon
- Beef meat pieces, one cup
- Soy sauce, one tablespoon
- Mongolian spice, two tablespoon
- Olive oil, two teaspoon

- Chopped garlic, one teaspoon
- Japanese fresh herbs, half teaspoon
- Fresh shiso leaves, two tablespoon
- Fresh cilantro leaves, half cup
- Chopped tomatoes, half cup
- Ramen, as required

Instructions:
1. Add the beef pieces into a pan.
2. Add the Mongolian spice and olive oil into the pan.
3. Cook the beef pieces for ten minutes or until they are completely cooked.
4. Dish out the beef pieces and shred them when cooled.
5. Take a large sauce pan.
6. Add all the ingredients of the sauce into the pan.
7. Add the shredded beef meat, nori paste, chopped tomatoes and the rest of the ingredients into the mixture.
8. Cook the dish for ten minutes.
9. Add the ramen into the mixture once the sauce is ready.
10. Mix the ramen well.
11. Cook the dish for five minutes.
12. Add the green onions into the dish.
13. Your dish is ready to be served.

3.15 Japanese Meatball Ramen Recipe

Preparation Time: 30 minutes
Cooking Time: 20 minutes
Serving: 4

Ingredients:

- Beef stock, two cups
- Crushed garlic, two
- Frozen bacon and beef meatballs, one pound
- Salt, to taste
- Black pepper, to taste
- Olive oil, two tablespoon
- Dried white wine, one cup
- Onion, one cup
- All-purpose flour, three tablespoon
- Worcestershire sauce, two tablespoon
- Softened butter, three tablespoon
- Bay leaf, one
- Fresh thyme, two tablespoon
- Grated or sliced cheese, one cup
- Chopped cilantro, one cup
- Ramen noodles, four packs

Instructions:

1. Take a large skillet.
2. Add the oil and onions into the skillet.
3. Cook the onions until they turn golden brown.
4. Add the crushed garlic into the skillet.
5. Add the spices into the mixture.
6. Add the all-purpose flour, Worcestershire sauce and dried white wine.
7. Add the butter and then add the beef stock and ramen noodles.
8. Fry the frozen meatballs in a pan full of cooking oil.
9. Dish out the meatballs when they turn golden brown on all sides.
10. Add the fried meatballs into the ramen mixture.
11. The dish is ready to be served.

3.16 Japanese Ramen Noodle Skillet with Steak Recipe

Preparation Time: 30 minutes

Cooking Time: 20 minutes
Serving: 4

Ingredients:

- Chicken stock, two cups
- Crushed garlic, two
- Steak meat, one pound
- Salt, to taste
- Black pepper, to taste
- Olive oil, two tablespoon
- Dried white wine, one cup
- Onion, one cup
- All-purpose flour, three tablespoon
- Worcestershire sauce, two tablespoon
- Softened butter, three tablespoon
- Bay leaf, one
- Fresh thyme, two tablespoon
- Grated or sliced cheese, one cup
- Chopped cilantro, one cup
- Ramen noodles, four packs

Instructions:

1. Take a large skillet.
2. Add the oil and onions into the skillet.
3. Cook the onions until they turn golden brown.
4. Add the crushed garlic into the skillet.
5. Add the spices into the mixture.
6. Add all-purpose flour, Worcestershire sauce and dried white wine.
7. Add the butter and then add the chicken stock and ramen noodles.
8. Grill the steak meat over a grill pan.
9. Cut the steak into long pieces.
10. Add the steak pieces on top of the ramen mixture.
11. Garnish the noodles with chopped cilantro.
12. The dish is ready to be served.

3.17 Japanese Cheese Ramen Recipe

Preparation Time: 30 minutes
Cooking Time: 20 minutes
Serving: 4

Ingredients:

- Mushroom sauce, one cup
- Miso paste, one teaspoon
- Onion, one cup

- Ramen noodles, four cups
- Shredded mozzarella cheese, one cup
- Water, one cup
- Bok choy, one cup
- Rice vinegar, one tablespoon
- Minced garlic, two tablespoon
- Minced ginger, two tablespoon
- Cilantro leaves, half cup
- Olive oil, two tablespoon
- Water, half cup
- Vegetable stock, half cup
- Chopped tomatoes, one cup

Instructions:
1. Take a pan.
2. Add in the oil and onions.
3. Cook the onions until they become soft and fragrant.
4. Add in the chopped garlic and ginger.
5. Cook the mixture and add the tomatoes into it.
6. Add the spices.
7. When the tomatoes are done, add the miso paste into it.
8. Mix the ingredients carefully and cover the pan.
9. Add the bok choy and rest of the ingredients.

10.   Add the water into the mixture and let the mixture boil.
11.   Add the ramen noodles into the mixture.
12.   Let the noodles cook for ten to fifteen minutes straight.
13.   Add cilantro leaves and shredded cheese on top.
14.   Your dish is ready to be served.

3.18 Japanese Ramen Burger Recipe

Preparation Time: 20 minutes
Cooking Time: 20 minutes
Serving: 4

Ingredients:

- Ramen buns, as required
- Minced beef meat, one cup
- Bread crumbs, one cup
- Egg, one
- Chopped parsley, half cup
- Fresh chopped cilantro, half cup
- Salt, to taste
- Black pepper, to taste
- Olive oil, for frying
- Yoghurt, half cup

- Lemon juice, a quarter cup
- Fresh chopped cilantro, two tablespoon
- Butter, one tablespoon

Instructions:
1. Take a large bowl.
2. Add the beef meat, salt, pepper, bread crumbs and egg into it.
3. Mix all the ingredients well.
4. Add the chopped cilantro and parsley into the mixture.
5. Mix the ingredients until they become smooth.
6. Shape the mixture into patties.
7. Add the olive oil in a large pan and cook the patties.
8. Cook the patties until they turn golden brown from both sides.
9. In the meanwhile, in a small bowl, add the yoghurt, lemon juice and fresh cilantro.
10. Mix it to form a paste.
11. Add butter on the ramen and heat them.
12. Add the beef patty on the ramen.
13. Add the paste on top of the patty and cover it with the ramen bun.
14. The ramen burger is ready to be served.

3.19 Japanese Garlic and Shrimp Ramen Recipe

Preparation Time: 20 minutes
Cooking Time: 20 minutes
Serving: 4

Ingredients:

- Ramen noodles, two packs
- Miso paste, one teaspoon
- Onion, one cup
- Shrimps, one pound
- Bell peppers, one cup
- Japanese fresh herbs, half teaspoon
- Water, one cup
- Minced garlic, two tablespoon
- Minced ginger, two tablespoon
- Cilantro, half cup
- Diced carrots, one cup
- Olive oil, two tablespoon
- Water, half cup
- Vegetable stock, two cups
- Chopped tomatoes, one cup

Instructions:
1. Take a pan.
2. Add in the oil and onions.
3. Cook the onions until they become soft and fragrant.
4. Add in the chopped garlic and ginger.
5. Cook the mixture and add the tomatoes into it.
6. Add the spices.
7. Add the miso paste into it when the tomatoes are done.
8. Mix the ingredients carefully and cover the pan.
9. Add the shrimps, vegetables and rest of the ingredients except the noodles.
10. Let the mixture boil.
11. Add the ramen noodles into the soup mixture.
12. Let the soup cook for ten to fifteen minutes straight.
13. Add cilantro on top.
14. Your dish is ready to be served.

3.20 Japanese Beef and Ramen Stir-Fry Recipe

Preparation Time: 30 minutes
Cooking Time: 10 minutes
Serving: 4

Ingredients:

- Ramen noodles, four packs
- Sesame oil, one tablespoon
- Cilantro, one cup
- Sesame seeds, half cup
- Fresh ginger, one teaspoon
- Dark soy sauce, one tablespoon
- Mirin paste, one tablespoon
- Dried shisho leaves, half teaspoon
- Chili garlic sauce, two tablespoon
- Thyme, one tablespoon
- Lemon zest, one teaspoon
- Lemon juice, half cup
- Beef pieces, one pound
- Fresh chopped garlic, half cup
- Fresh basil leaves, a quarter cup
- Vegetable broth, one cup

Instructions:
1. Boil the ramen noodles.
2. Add all the ingredients of the sauce into a wok.
3. Cook the ingredients.
4. Add the beef pieces, lemon juice, thyme, lemon zest and rest of the ingredients into the mixture.

5. Add the ramen noodles into the mixture once the mixture is ready.
6. Mix the ramen noodles well and cook it for five minutes.
7. Add the cilantro into the dish.
8. Your dish is ready to be served.

Chapter 4: The World of Ramen Dinner Recipes

Ramen dinner recipes are well- known all over the world for its mesmerizing flavors and varieties. Following are some amazing and healthy Ramen dinner recipes that you would love to make at home:

4.1 Japanese Parmesan and Garlic Ramen Recipe

Preparation Time: 20 minutes

Cooking Time: 20 minutes

Serving: 4

Ingredients:

- Parmesan cheese, one cup
- Ramen noodles, two packs
- Miso paste, one teaspoon
- Onion, one cup
- Bell peppers, one cup
- Japanese fresh herbs, half teaspoon
- Water, one cup
- Minced garlic, two tablespoon
- Cilantro, half cup
- Diced carrots, one cup

- Olive oil, two tablespoon
- Water, half cup
- Vegetable stock, two cups
- Chopped tomatoes, one cup

Instructions:
1. Take a pan.
2. Add in the oil and onions.
3. Cook the onions until they become soft and fragrant.
4. Add in the chopped garlic.
5. Cook the mixture and add the tomatoes into it.
6. Add the spices.
7. Add the miso paste into it when the tomatoes are done.
8. Mix the ingredients carefully and cover the pan.
9. Add the vegetables and rest of the ingredients except the noodles and parmesan cheese.
10. Let the mixture boil.
11. Add the ramen noodles into the soup mixture.
12. Let the soup cook for ten to fifteen minutes straight.
13. Add cilantro and parmesan cheese on top.
14. Your dish is ready to be served.

4.2 Japanese Ginger and Beef Stir-Fry Ramen Recipe

Preparation Time: 30 minutes
Cooking Time: 10 minutes
Serving: 4

Ingredients:

- Ramen noodles, four packs
- Sesame oil, one tablespoon
- Cilantro, one cup
- Sesame seeds, half cup
- Fresh ginger, two tablespoon
- Dark soy sauce, one tablespoon
- Mirin paste, one tablespoon
- Dried shisho leaves, half teaspoon
- Chili garlic sauce, two tablespoon
- Thyme, one tablespoon
- Lemon zest, one teaspoon
- Lemon juice, half cup
- Beef pieces, one pound
- Fresh basil leaves, a quarter cup
- Vegetable broth, one cup

Instructions:
1. Boil the ramen noodles.
2. Add all the ingredients of the sauce into a wok.
3. Cook the ingredients.
4. Add the beef pieces, chopped ginger, lemon juice, thyme, lemon zest and rest of the ingredients into the mixture.
5. Add the ramen noodles into the mixture once the mixture is ready.
6. Mix the ramen noodles well and cook it for five minutes.
7. Add the cilantro into the dish.
8. Your dish is ready to be served.

4.3 Japanese Peanut and Chicken Ramen Recipe

Preparation Time: 30 minutes
Cooking Time: 20 minutes
Serving: 4

Ingredients:

- Mushroom sauce, one cup
- Miso paste, one teaspoon
- Onion, one cup
- Ramen noodles, four cups
- Peanuts, one cup

- Water, one cup
- Chicken pieces, one cup
- Rice vinegar, one tablespoon
- Minced garlic, two tablespoon
- Minced ginger, two tablespoon
- Cilantro leaves, half cup
- Olive oil, two tablespoon
- Water, half cup
- Chicken stock, half cup
- Chopped tomatoes, one cup

Instructions:
1. Take a pan.
2. Add in the oil and onions.
3. Cook the onions until they become soft and fragrant.
4. Add in the chopped garlic and ginger.
5. Cook the mixture and add the tomatoes into it.
6. Add the spices.
7. When the tomatoes are done, add the chicken stock, and miso paste into it.
8. Mix the ingredients carefully and cover the pan.
9. Add the chicken and rest of the ingredients.
10. Add the water into the mixture and let the mixture boil.
11. Add the ramen noodles into the mixture.

12. Let the soup cook for ten to fifteen minutes straight.
13. Add cilantro leaves and peanuts on top.
14. Your dish is ready to be served.

4.4 Japanese Roasted Chicken Ramen Recipe

Preparation Time: 30 minutes
Cooking Time: 20 minutes
Serving: 4

Ingredients:

- Chicken stock, two cups
- Crushed garlic, two
- Chicken pieces, one pound
- Salt, to taste
- Black pepper, to taste
- Olive oil, two tablespoon
- Dried white wine, one cup
- Onion, one cup
- All-purpose flour, three tablespoon
- Worcestershire sauce, two tablespoon
- Softened butter, three tablespoon
- Bay leaf, one

- Fresh thyme, two tablespoon
- Grated or sliced cheese, one cup
- Chopped cilantro, one cup
- Ramen noodles, four packs

Instructions:
1. Take a large skillet.
2. Add the oil and onions into the skillet.
3. Cook the onions until they turn golden brown.
4. Add the crushed garlic into the skillet.
5. Add the spices into the mixture.
6. Add the all-purpose flour, Worcestershire sauce and dried white wine.
7. Add the butter and then add the chicken stock and ramen noodles.
8. Roast the chicken pieces in a preheated oven.
9. Cut the chicken into long pieces.
10. Add the chicken into the ramen mixture.
11. The dish is ready to be served.

4.5 Japanese Sirarcha and Shrimp Ramen Recipe

Preparation Time: 20 minutes
Cooking Time: 20 minutes
Serving: 4

Ingredients:

- Ramen noodles, two packs
- Miso paste, one teaspoon
- Onion, one cup
- Shrimps, one pound
- Bell peppers, one cup
- Japanese fresh herbs, half teaspoon
- Water, one cup
- Minced garlic, two tablespoon
- Minced ginger, two tablespoon
- Cilantro, half cup
- Diced carrots, one cup
- Olive oil, two tablespoon
- Sirarcha sauce, half cup
- Fish stock, two cups
- Chopped tomatoes, one cup

Instructions:
1. Take a pan.
2. Add in the oil and onions.
3. Cook the onions until they become soft and fragrant.
4. Add in the chopped garlic and ginger.
5. Cook the mixture and add the tomatoes into it.
6. Add the spices.
7. Add the miso paste and sirarcha into it when the tomatoes are done.
8. Mix the ingredients carefully and cover the pan.
9. Add the shrimps, vegetables and rest of the ingredients except the noodles.
10. Let the mixture boil.
11. Add the ramen noodles into the soup mixture.
12. Let the soup cook for ten to fifteen minutes straight.
13. Add cilantro on top.
14. Your dish is ready to be served.

4.6 Japanese Bacon Ramen Soup Recipe

Preparation Time: 20 minutes
Cooking Time: 20 minutes
Serving: 4

Ingredients:

- Ramen noodles, two packs
- Miso paste, one teaspoon
- Onion, one cup
- Chopped bacon, one cup
- Japanese fresh herbs, half teaspoon
- Water, one cup
- Minced garlic, two tablespoon
- Minced ginger, two tablespoon
- Cilantro, half cup
- Olive oil, two tablespoon
- Water, half cup
- Chicken stock, two cups
- Chopped tomatoes, one cup

Instructions:
1. Take a pan.

2. Add in the oil and onions.
3. Cook the onions until they become soft and fragrant.
4. Add in the chopped garlic and ginger.
5. Cook the mixture and add the tomatoes into it.
6. Add the spices.
7. Add the chopped bacon into it when the tomatoes are done.
8. Mix the ingredients carefully and cover the pan.
9. Add the rest of the ingredients except the noodles.
10. Let the mixture boil.
11. Add the ramen noodles into the soup mixture.
12. Let the soup cook for ten to fifteen minutes straight.
13. Add cilantro on top.
14. Your dish is ready to be served.

4.7 Japanese Sweet and Sour Pork Ramen Recipe

Preparation Time: 30 minutes
Cooking Time: 10 minutes
Serving: 4

Ingredients:

- Sweet and sour sauce, one cup
- Chili paste, two tablespoon
- Sliced green onions, half cup
- Mirin paste, one teaspoon
- Fresh ginger, one teaspoon
- Miso paste, one tablespoon
- Cooked and shredded pork meat, one cup
- Soy sauce, one tablespoon
- Japanese fresh herbs, half teaspoon
- Fresh shiso leaves, two tablespoon
- Fresh cilantro leaves, half cup
- Chopped tomatoes, half cup
- Ramen, as required

Instructions:

1. Add all the ingredients of the sauce i.e. miso paste, soy sauce, mirin paste and Japanese fresh herbs into a large pan.
2. Add the shredded pork meat, sweet and sour sauce, chopped tomatoes and the rest of the ingredients into the mixture.
3. Cook the dish for ten minutes.
4. Add the ramen into the mixture once the sauce is ready.
5. Mix the ramen well.
6. Cook the dish for five minutes.
7. Add the green onions into the dish.
8. Your dish is ready to be served.

4.8 Japanese Cheesy Tuna Ramen Recipe

Preparation Time: 30 minutes
Cooking Time: 20 minutes
Serving: 4

Ingredients:

- Miso paste, one teaspoon
- Onion, one cup
- Ramen noodles, four cups
- Shredded mozzarella cheese, one cup
- Water, one cup
- Tuna pieces, one cup

- Rice vinegar, one tablespoon
- Minced garlic, two tablespoon
- Minced ginger, two tablespoon
- Cilantro leaves, half cup
- Olive oil, two tablespoon
- Water, half cup
- Fish stock, half cup
- Chopped tomatoes, one cup

Instructions:
1. Take a pan.
2. Add in the oil and onions.
3. Cook the onions until they become soft and fragrant.
4. Add in the chopped garlic and ginger.
5. Cook the mixture and add the tomatoes into it.
6. Add the spices.
7. When the tomatoes are done, add the miso paste into it.
8. Mix the ingredients carefully and cover the pan.
9. Add the tuna pieces and rest of the ingredients.
10. Add the water into the mixture and let the mixture boil.
11. Add the ramen noodles into the mixture.
12. Let the noodles cook for ten to fifteen minutes straight.

13. Add cilantro leaves and shredded cheese on top.
14. Your dish is ready to be served.

4.9 Japanese Ramen and Tomato Soup Recipe

Preparation Time: 30 minutes
Cooking Time: 10 minutes
Serving: 4

Ingredients:

- Tomato paste, one cup
- Sliced green onions, half cup
- Mirin paste, one teaspoon
- Cilantro, one cup
- Fresh ginger, one teaspoon
- Miso paste, one tablespoon
- Soy sauce, one tablespoon
- Japanese fresh herbs, half teaspoon
- Fresh shiso leaves, two tablespoon
- Fresh cilantro leaves, half cup
- Chopped tomatoes, half cup
- Ramen, as required

Instructions:

1. Add all the ingredients of the sauce i.e. miso paste, soy sauce, mirin paste and Japanese fresh herbs into a large pan.
2. Add the tomato paste, chopped tomatoes and the rest of the ingredients into the mixture.
3. Cook the dish for ten minutes.
4. Add the ramen into the mixture once the sauce is ready.
5. Mix the ramen well.
6. Cook the dish for five minutes.
7. Add the cilantro and the green onions into the dish.
8. Your dish is ready to be served.

4.10 Japanese Chili Ramen Recipe

Preparation Time: 20 minutes

Cooking Time: 20 minutes

Serving: 4

Ingredients:

- Ramen noodles, two packs
- Miso paste, one teaspoon
- Onion, one cup
- Chili paste, one tablespoon
- Japanese fresh herbs, half teaspoon

- Water, one cup
- Minced garlic, two tablespoon
- Cilantro, half cup
- Chopped green chilies, one cup
- Olive oil, two tablespoon
- Vegetable stock, two cups
- Chopped tomatoes, one cup

Instructions:
1. Take a pan.
2. Add in the oil and onions.
3. Cook the onions until they become soft and fragrant.
4. Add in the chopped garlic.
5. Cook the mixture and add the tomatoes into it.
6. Add the spices.
7. Add the chili paste into it when the tomatoes are done.
8. Mix the ingredients carefully and cover the pan.
9. Add the chopped green chilies and rest of the ingredients except the noodles.
10. Let the mixture boil.
11. Add the ramen noodles into the mixture.
12. Let the ingredients cook for ten to fifteen minutes straight.
13. Add cilantro on top.
14. Your dish is ready to be served.

4.11 Japanese Chicken and Mushroom Ramen Recipe

Preparation Time: 20 minutes
Cooking Time: 20 minutes
Serving: 4

Ingredients:

- Ramen noodles, two packs
- Miso paste, one teaspoon
- Onion, one cup
- Chicken pieces, one cup
- Japanese fresh herbs, half teaspoon
- Water, one cup
- Minced garlic, two tablespoon
- Cilantro, half cup
- Sliced mushrooms, one cup
- Olive oil, two tablespoon
- Water, half cup
- Chicken stock, two cups
- Chopped tomatoes, one cup

Instructions:
1. Take a pan.
2. Add in the oil and onions.
3. Cook the onions until they become soft and fragrant.
4. Add in the chopped garlic.
5. Cook the mixture and add the tomatoes into it.
6. Add the spices.
7. Add the chicken pieces into it when the tomatoes are done.
8. Mix the ingredients carefully and cover the pan.
9. Add the mushrooms and rest of the ingredients except the noodles.
10. Let the mixture boil.
11. Add the ramen noodles into the soup mixture.
12. Let the soup cook for ten to fifteen minutes straight.
13. Add cilantro on top.
14. Your dish is ready to be served.

4.12 Japanese Parmesan Chicken Ramen Recipe

Preparation Time: 20 minutes
Cooking Time: 20 minutes
Serving: 4

Ingredients:

- Parmesan cheese, one cup
- Ramen noodles, two packs
- Miso paste, one teaspoon
- Onion, one cup
- Chicken pieces, one cup
- Japanese fresh herbs, half teaspoon
- Water, one cup
- Minced garlic, two tablespoon
- Cilantro, half cup
- Olive oil, two tablespoon
- Water, half cup
- Chicken stock, two cups
- Chopped tomatoes, one cup

Instructions:
1. Take a pan.
2. Add in the oil and onions.
3. Cook the onions until they become soft and fragrant.
4. Add in the chopped garlic.
5. Cook the mixture and add the tomatoes into it.
6. Add the spices.
7. Add the miso paste into it when the tomatoes are done.

8. Add the chicken pieces and rest of the ingredients except the noodles and parmesan cheese.
9. Let the mixture boil.
10. Add the ramen noodles into the soup mixture.
11. Let the soup cook for ten to fifteen minutes straight.
12. Add cilantro and parmesan cheese on top.
13. Your dish is ready to be served.

4.13 Japanese Chicken Lo Mein Ramen Recipe

Preparation Time: 30 minutes

Cooking Time: 10 minutes

Serving: 4

Ingredients:

- Diced cabbage, one cup
- Brown sugar, two tablespoon
- Sliced green onions, half cup
- Mirin paste, one teaspoon
- Fresh ginger, one teaspoon
- Miso paste, one tablespoon
- Cooked and shredded chicken meat, one cup

- Soy sauce, one tablespoon
- Shiitake mushrooms, one cup
- Japanese fresh herbs, half teaspoon
- Fresh shiso leaves, two tablespoon
- Fresh cilantro leaves, half cup
- Chopped tomatoes, half cup
- Ramen, as required

Instructions:

1. Add all the ingredients of the sauce i.e. miso paste, soy sauce, mirin paste and Japanese fresh herbs into a large pan.
2. Add the shredded chicken, diced cabbage, brown sugar, shitake mushrooms and the rest of the ingredients into the mixture.
3. Cook the dish for ten minutes.
4. Add the ramen into the mixture once the sauce is ready.
5. Mix the ramen well.
6. Cook the dish for five minutes.
7. Add the green onions into the dish.
8. Your dish is ready to be served.

4.14 Japanese Shrimp Ramen Recipe

Preparation Time: 30 minutes
Cooking Time: 10 minutes

Serving: 4

Ingredients:

- Shiitake mushrooms, one cup
- Diced carrots, one cup
- Sliced green onions, half cup
- Mirin paste, one teaspoon
- Fresh ginger, one teaspoon
- Miso paste, one tablespoon
- Devilled shrimps, one cup
- Soy sauce, one tablespoon
- Chopped garlic, one teaspoon
- Japanese fresh herbs, half teaspoon
- Fresh shiso leaves, two tablespoon
- Fresh cilantro leaves, half cup
- Chopped tomatoes, half cup
- Ramen, as required

Instructions:

1. Add all the ingredients of the sauce i.e. miso paste, soy sauce, mirin paste and Japanese fresh herbs into a large pan.

2. Add the devilled shrimps, carrots, mushrooms, chopped tomatoes and the rest of the ingredients into the mixture.
3. Cook the dish for ten minutes.
4. Add the ramen into the mixture once the sauce is ready.
5. Mix the ramen well.
6. Cook the dish for five minutes.
7. Add the green onions into the dish.
8. Your dish is ready to be served.

4.15 Japanese Green Pepper and Chicken Ramen Recipe

Preparation Time: 20 minutes

Cooking Time: 20 minutes

Serving: 4

Ingredients:

- Ramen noodles, two packs
- Miso paste, one teaspoon
- Onion, one cup
- Chicken pieces, one cup
- Japanese fresh herbs, half teaspoon
- Water, one cup
- Minced garlic, two tablespoon

- Cilantro, half cup
- Green pepper, one cup
- Olive oil, two tablespoon
- Water, half cup
- Chicken stock, two cups
- Chopped tomatoes, one cup

Instructions:
1. Take a pan.
2. Add in the oil and onions.
3. Cook the onions until they become soft and fragrant.
4. Add in the chopped garlic.
5. Cook the mixture and add the tomatoes into it.
6. Add the spices.
7. Add the chicken pieces into it when the tomatoes are done.
8. Mix the ingredients carefully and cover the pan.
9. Add the green pepper and rest of the ingredients except the noodles.
10. Let the mixture boil.
11. Add the ramen noodles into the soup mixture.
12. Let the soup cook for ten to fifteen minutes straight.
13. Add cilantro on top.
14. Your dish is ready to be served.

4.16 Japanese Creamy Tonkotsu Ramen Recipe

Preparation time: 30 minutes
Cooking Time: 10 minutes
Serving: 4

Ingredients:

- Heavy cream, one cup
- Sliced green onions, half cup
- Mirin paste, one teaspoon
- Cilantro, one cup
- Fresh ginger, one teaspoon
- Miso paste, one tablespoon
- Soy sauce, one tablespoon
- Japanese fresh herbs, half teaspoon
- Chopped leeks, two tablespoon
- Chicken meat, one cup
- Tonkatsu broth, one cup
- Fresh cilantro leaves, half cup
- Minced lemon grass, one teaspoon
- Ramen, as required

Instructions:

1. Add all the ingredients of the sauce i.e. miso paste, soy sauce, mirin paste and Japanese fresh herbs into a large pan.
2. Add the heavy cream and the rest of the ingredients into the mixture.
3. Cook the dish for ten minutes.
4. Add the ramen into the mixture once the sauce is ready.
5. Mix the ramen well.
6. Close the lid of the instant pot.
7. Cook the dish for five more minutes.
8. Add the cilantro into the dish.
9. Your dish is ready to be served.

4.17 Japanese Miso and Crispy Pork Ramen Recipe

Preparation Time: 20 minutes

Cooking Time: 10 minutes

Serving: 4

Ingredients:

- Miso paste, half cup
- Sliced green onions, half cup
- Mirin paste, one teaspoon
- Cilantro, one cup

- Fresh ginger, one teaspoon
- Soy sauce, one tablespoon
- Japanese fresh herbs, half teaspoon
- Fresh shiso leaves, two tablespoon
- Fresh cilantro leaves, half cup
- Minced lemon grass, one teaspoon
- Ramen, as required
- Pork strips, one cup
- Corn starch, two teaspoon
- Cooking oil, as required

Instructions:
1. Heat a large pan.
2. Add the cooking oil and let it heat.
3. Mix the pork and cornstarch and add it into the heated oil.
4. Cook the pork well for about five minutes.
5. Dish out the pork strips and set aside when done.
6. Add the miso paste and the rest of the ingredients into the mixture.
7. Cook the ingredients for ten minutes.
8. Add the ramen into the mixture once the sauce is ready.
9. Mix the ramen well.
10. Cook the dish for five minutes.
11. Add the crispy pork on top.

12. Add the cilantro into the dish.
13. Your dish is ready to be served.

4.18 Japanese Shio and Pork Ramen Recipe

Preparation Time: 20 minutes
Cooking Time: 20 minutes
Serving: 4

Ingredients:

- Ramen noodles, two packs
- Cooked and shredded pork, one cup
- Spicy chili bean sauce, two teaspoon
- Onion, one cup
- Dashi stock, two cups
- Japanese fresh herbs, half teaspoon
- Water, one cup
- Minced garlic, two tablespoon
- Minced ginger, two tablespoon
- Cilantro, half cup
- Chili oil, two tablespoon
- Shredded nori sheets, half cup
- Sheragi negi, two cups
- Chopped tomatoes, one cup

Instructions:
1. Take a pan.
2. Add in the oil and onions.
3. Cook the onions until they become soft and fragrant.
4. Add in the chopped garlic and ginger.
5. Cook the mixture for a few seconds.
6. Add the spices.
7. Add the sgeragi negi and shredded pork into it when the spices are done.
8. Mix the ingredients carefully and cover the pan.
9. Let the mixture boil.
10. Add the ramen noodles into the soup mixture.
11. Let the soup cook for ten to fifteen minutes straight.
12. Add shredded nori sheets on top.
13. Your dish is ready to be served.

4.19 Japanese Ramen Noodle Coleslaw Recipe

Preparation Time: 20 minutes
Cooking Time: 40 minutes
Serving: 2

Ingredients:

- Coleslaw mix, two cups
- Maple syrup, half teaspoon
- Sesame oil, one teaspoon
- Soy sauce, one teaspoon
- Salt, to taste
- Ramen noodles, four packs
- Pepper, to taste

Instructions:
1. Boil the ramen noodles in a large pot full of water.
2. Drain the noodles when they are cooked.
3. Take a large bowl and add boiled noodles into it.
4. Add the rest of the ingredients into the bowl.
5. Add the salt and pepper as you like.
6. Add the sesame oil and mix well so that a consistent mixture is obtained.
7. The salad is ready to be served.

4.20 Japanese Instant Ramen Noodle Recipe

Preparation Time: 10 minutes
Cooking Time: 10 minutes
Serving: 4

Ingredients:

- Water, two cups
- Ramen noodles, two pack
- Mirin paste, one tablespoon
- Mix spice, half cup
- Dashi powder, two tablespoon
- Fresh shiso leaves, a quarter cup
- Sesame oil, one tablespoon

Instructions:
1. Take a large pan.
2. Add all the ingredients into the pan.
3. Cook the ingredients for ten minutes.
4. Garnish it with shiso leaves.
5. Your dish is ready to be served.

Chapter 5: The World of Vegetarian Ramen Recipes

Ramen noodles are a comfort food for everyone in the world. It tends to be straightforward and economical, and you can make it extravagant and jam-loaded with beautiful and healthy vegetables and flavors. You should try all of these twenty yummy vegetarian recipes at home as they are easy to make and will surely make your day:

5.1 Japanese Spicy Vegetarian Ramen Recipe

Preparation Time: 30 minutes

Cooking Time: 10 minutes

Serving: 4

Ingredients:

- Chili paste, two tablespoon
- Sliced green onions, half cup
- Mirin paste, one teaspoon
- Fresh ginger, one teaspoon
- Miso paste, one tablespoon
- Chopped carrots, one cup
- Soy sauce, one tablespoon
- Shredded zucchini, one cup
- Blanched peas, one cup

- Chopped garlic, one teaspoon
- Japanese fresh herbs, half teaspoon
- Fresh shiso leaves, two tablespoon
- Fresh cilantro leaves, half cup
- Chopped tomatoes, half cup
- Ramen, as required

Instructions:
1. Add all the ingredients of the sauce i.e. miso paste, soy sauce, mirin paste and Japanese fresh herbs into a large pan.
2. Add the vegetables, chili paste, chopped tomatoes and the rest of the ingredients into the mixture.
3. Cook the dish for ten minutes.
4. Add the ramen into the mixture once the sauce is ready.
5. Mix the ramen well.
6. Cook the dish for five minutes.
7. Add the green onions into the dish.
8. Your dish is ready to be served.

5.2 Japanese Shiitake Mushroom Ramen Recipe

Preparation Time: 30 minutes

Cooking Time: 10 minutes

Serving: 4

Ingredients:

- Bean sprouts, one cup
- Sliced green onions, half cup
- Mirin paste, one teaspoon
- Cilantro, one cup
- Bamboo shoots, one teaspoon
- Miso paste, one tablespoon
- Shiitake mushrooms, one cup
- Soy sauce, one tablespoon
- Cooking oil, two tablespoon
- Chopped garlic, one teaspoon
- Japanese fresh herbs, half teaspoon
- Fresh shiso leaves, two tablespoon
- Fresh cilantro leaves, half cup
- Dried chili flakes, two teaspoon
- Soft boiled eggs, four
- Ramen, as required

Instructions:
1. Take a large pan.
2. Add the cooking oil and chopped garlic into the pan.
3. Add the shiitake mushrooms into the pan.

4. Add all the spices into the mixture.
5. Cook the ingredients for five minutes.
6. Add the bean sprouts and ramen into the mixture.
7. Cook all the ingredients well.
8. Peel the soft boiled eggs and add them into the mixture.
9. Cook for five minutes.
10. Garnish the dish with cilantro and green onions.
11. Your dish is ready to be served.

5.3 Japanese Miso Vegetarian Ramen Noodle Soup Recipe

Preparation Time: 20 minutes
Cooking Time: 20 minutes
Serving: 4

Ingredients:

- Ramen noodles, two packs
- Miso paste, one teaspoon
- Onion, one cup
- Bean sprouts, one cup
- Japanese fresh herbs, half teaspoon
- Water, one cup

- Minced garlic, two tablespoon
- Minced ginger, two tablespoon
- Cilantro, half cup
- Diced carrots, one cup
- Olive oil, two tablespoon
- Blanched peas, half cup
- Vegetable stock, two cups
- Chopped tomatoes, one cup

Instructions:
1. Take a pan.
2. Add in the oil and onions.
3. Cook the onions until they become soft and fragrant.
4. Add in the chopped garlic and ginger.
5. Cook the mixture and add the tomatoes into it.
6. Add the spices.
7. Add the miso paste into it when the tomatoes are done.
8. Mix the ingredients carefully and cover the pan.
9. Add the carrot, peas, bean sprouts and rest of the ingredients except the noodles.
10. Let the mixture boil.
11. Add the ramen noodles into the soup mixture.
12. Let the soup cook for ten to fifteen minutes straight.

13. Add cilantro on top.
14. Your dish is ready to be served.

5.4 Japanese Teriyaki Tofu Ramen Recipe

Preparation Time: 30 minutes
Cooking Time: 10 minutes
Serving: 4

Ingredients:

- Teriyaki sauce, one cup
- Sliced green onions, half cup
- Mirin paste, one teaspoon
- Cilantro, one cup
- Bamboo shoots, one teaspoon
- Miso paste, one tablespoon
- Soy sauce, one tablespoon
- Cooking oil, two tablespoon
- Chopped garlic, one teaspoon
- Japanese fresh herbs, half teaspoon
- Fresh shiso leaves, two tablespoon
- Fresh cilantro leaves, half cup
- Dried chili flakes, two teaspoon
- Tofu cubes, one cup

- Ramen, as required

Instructions:
1. Take a large pan.
2. Add the cooking oil and chopped garlic into the pan.
3. Add the tofu cubes into the pan.
4. Add all the spices into the mixture.
5. Cook the ingredients for five minutes.
6. Add the teriyaki sauce and ramen into the mixture.
7. Cook all the ingredients well.
8. Cover the pan for five minutes.
9. Garnish the dish with cilantro and green onions.
10. Your dish is ready to be served.

5.5 Japanese Tonkotsu Vegetarian Ramen Recipe

Preparation Time: 30 minutes

Cooking Time: 10 minutes

Serving: 4

Ingredients:

- Chopped chives, one teaspoon

- Butter, two tablespoon
- Tonkotsu broth, one cup
- Salt, to taste
- Black pepper, to taste
- Tamari paste, two teaspoon
- Mix vegetables, two cups
- Mirin paste, one tablespoon
- Chopped garlic, one teaspoon
- Ramen noodles, four packs

Instructions:
1. Take a large pan.
2. Add the butter and let it meltdown.
3. Add in the tamari paste.
4. Mix the tamari paste for two minutes.
5. Add the chopped garlic and mixed vegetables.
6. Add in the salt and pepper.
7. Add in the tonkotsu broth and rest of the ingredients in the end.
8. Mix all the ingredients well and then dish them out.
9. Garnish the fresh chopped chives on top.
10. Your dish is ready to be served.

5.6 Japanese Pantry Vegetarian Ramen Recipe

Preparation Time: 10 minutes
Cooking Time: 10 minutes
Serving: 4

Ingredients:

- Garlic powder, one teaspoon
- Soy sauce, a quarter cup
- Sliced green onions, half cup
- Ginger powder, one teaspoon
- Lemon juice, half cup
- Miso paste, one tablespoon
- Sirarcha sauce, two tablespoon
- Vegetables (of your choice), one cup
- Japanese fresh herbs, half teaspoon
- Ketchup, two tablespoon
- Fresh cilantro leaves, half cup
- Sliced scallions, half cup
- Ramen, as required
- Sesame oil, two tablespoon

Instructions:

1. Take a large saucepan.
2. Add the sesame oil and scallions into the pan.
3. Cook the scallions for a few minutes.
4. Add the garlic powder.
5. Add the ketchup and sirarcha into the mixture.
6. Cook the ingredients for two minutes.
7. Add the vegetables of your choice into the pan.
8. Cook the ingredients well.
9. Add the rest of the ingredients along with the ramen noodles.
10. Cook the mixture for ten minutes.
11. Garnish the ramen with green onions and cilantro on top.
12. Your dish is ready to be served.

5.7 Japanese Marinated Tofu and Vegetable Ramen Recipe

Preparation Time: 30 minutes

Cooking Time: 20 minutes

Serving: 4

Ingredients:

- Vegetable stock, two cups
- Crushed garlic, two
- Tofu cubes, one pound

- Salt, to taste
- Black pepper, to taste
- Olive oil, two tablespoon
- Dried white wine, one cup
- Onion, one cup
- All-purpose flour, three tablespoon
- Worcestershire sauce, two tablespoon
- Softened butter, three tablespoon
- Bay leaf, one
- Fresh thyme, two tablespoon
- Soy sauce, one cup
- Chopped cilantro, one cup
- Ramen noodles, four packs

Instructions:
1. Marinate the tofu cubes in soy sauce for ten to fifteen minutes.
2. Take a large skillet.
3. Add the oil and onions into the skillet.
4. Cook the onions until they turn golden brown.
5. Add the crushed garlic into the skillet.
6. Add the spices into the mixture.
7. Add all-purpose flour, Worcestershire sauce and dried white wine.
8. Add the butter and then add the vegetable stock and ramen noodles.

9. Add the tofu cubes into the ramen mixture.
10. Cook the mixture for ten minutes.
11. The dish is ready to be served.

5.8 Japanese Creamy Vegan Ramen Recipe

Preparation Time: 30 minutes
Cooking Time: 10 minutes
Serving: 4

Ingredients:

- Heavy cream, one cup
- Sliced green onions, half cup
- Mirin paste, one teaspoon
- Cilantro, one cup
- Fresh ginger, one teaspoon
- Miso paste, one tablespoon
- Soy sauce, one tablespoon
- Japanese fresh herbs, half teaspoon
- Chopped leeks, two tablespoon
- Tonkatsu broth, one cup
- Fresh cilantro leaves, half cup
- Minced lemon grass, one teaspoon
- Ramen, as required

Instructions:

1. Add all the ingredients of the sauce i.e. miso paste, soy sauce, mirin paste and Japanese fresh herbs into a large pan.
2. Add the heavy cream and the rest of the ingredients into the mixture.
3. Cook the dish for ten minutes.
4. Add the ramen into the mixture once the sauce is ready.
5. Mix the ramen well.
6. Close the lid of the instant pot.
7. Cook the dish for five more minutes.
8. Add the cilantro into the dish.
9. Your dish is ready to be served.

5.9 Japanese Creamy Sesame Ramen Broth Recipe

Preparation Time: 20 minutes

Cooking Time: 20 minutes

Serving: 4

Ingredients:

- Ramen noodles, two packs
- Miso paste, one teaspoon

- Onion, one cup
- Sesame seeds, one cup
- Japanese fresh herbs, half teaspoon
- Water, one cup
- Minced garlic, two tablespoon
- Minced ginger, two tablespoon
- Cilantro, half cup
- Heavy cream, one cup
- Olive oil, two tablespoon
- Water, half cup
- Vegetable stock, two cups
- Chopped tomatoes, one cup

Instructions:
1. Take a pan.
2. Add in the oil and onions.
3. Cook the onions until they become soft and fragrant.
4. Add in the chopped garlic and ginger.
5. Cook the mixture and add the tomatoes into it.
6. Add the spices.
7. Add the miso paste into it when the tomatoes are done.
8. Mix the ingredients carefully and cover the pan.
9. Add the sesame seeds and the rest of the ingredients except the noodles.

10. Let the mixture boil.
11. Add the ramen noodles and heavy cream into the broth mixture.
12. Let the broth cook for ten to fifteen minutes straight.
13. Add cilantro on top.
14. Your dish is ready to be served.

5.10 Japanese Spicy Broccoli Ramen Recipe

Preparation Time: 30 minutes
Cooking Time: 10 minutes
Serving: 4

Ingredients:

- Chili paste, two tablespoon
- Sliced green onions, half cup
- Mirin paste, one teaspoon
- Fresh ginger, one teaspoon
- Miso paste, one tablespoon
- Chopped broccoli, one cup
- Soy sauce, one tablespoon
- Chopped garlic, one teaspoon
- Japanese fresh herbs, half teaspoon
- Fresh shiso leaves, two tablespoon

- Fresh cilantro leaves, half cup
- Chopped tomatoes, half cup
- Ramen, as required

Instructions:

1. Add all the ingredients of the sauce i.e. miso paste, soy sauce, mirin paste and Japanese fresh herbs into a large pan.
2. Add the broccoli, chili paste, chopped tomatoes and the rest of the ingredients into the mixture.
3. Cook the dish for ten minutes.
4. Add the ramen into the mixture once the sauce is ready.
5. Mix the ramen well.
6. Cook the dish for five minutes.
7. Add the green onions into the dish.
8. Your dish is ready to be served.

5.11 Japanese Cauliflower Ramen Recipe

Preparation Time: 20 minutes
Cooking Time: 10 minutes
Serving: 4

Ingredients:

- Miso paste, half cup
- Sliced green onions, half cup
- Cauliflower florets, two cups
- Cilantro, one cup
- Fresh ginger, one teaspoon
- Soy sauce, one tablespoon
- Japanese fresh herbs, half teaspoon
- Fresh shiso leaves, two tablespoon
- Fresh cilantro leaves, half cup
- Minced lemon grass, one teaspoon
- Ramen, as required

Instructions:
1. Heat a large pan.
2. Add the cauliflower florets and the rest of the ingredients into the mixture.
3. Cook the ingredients for ten minutes.
4. Add the ramen into the mixture once the sauce is ready.
5. Mix the ramen well.
6. Cook the dish for five minutes.
7. Add the cilantro into the dish.
8. Your dish is ready to be served.

5.12 Japanese Hot and Sour Dashi Ramen Recipe

Preparation Time: 30 minutes
Cooking Time: 10 minutes
Serving: 4

Ingredients:

- Hot and sour sauce, one cup
- Sliced green onions, half cup
- Mirin paste, one teaspoon
- Fresh ginger, one teaspoon
- Miso paste, one tablespoon
- Dashi stock, one cup
- Soy sauce, one tablespoon
- Japanese fresh herbs, half teaspoon
- Fresh shiso leaves, two tablespoon
- Fresh cilantro leaves, half cup
- Chopped tomatoes, half cup
- Ramen, as required

Instructions:
1. Add all the ingredients of the sauce i.e. miso paste, soy sauce, mirin paste and Japanese fresh herbs into a large pan.

2. Add the dashi stock, hot and sour sauce, chopped tomatoes and the rest of the ingredients into the mixture.
3. Cook the dish for ten minutes.
4. Add the ramen into the mixture once the sauce is ready.
5. Mix the ramen well.
6. Cook the dish for five minutes.
7. Add the green onions into the dish.
8. Your dish is ready to be served.

5.13 Japanese Spicy Carrot Ramen Recipe

Preparation Time: 30 minutes
Cooking Time: 10 minutes
Serving: 4

Ingredients:

- Chili paste, two tablespoon
- Sliced green onions, half cup
- Mirin paste, one teaspoon
- Fresh ginger, one teaspoon
- Miso paste, one tablespoon
- Chopped carrots, one cup
- Soy sauce, one tablespoon
- Chopped garlic, one teaspoon

- Japanese fresh herbs, half teaspoon
- Fresh shiso leaves, two tablespoon
- Fresh cilantro leaves, half cup
- Chopped tomatoes, half cup
- Ramen, as required

Instructions:

1. Add all the ingredients of the sauce i.e. miso paste, soy sauce, mirin paste and Japanese fresh herbs into a large pan.
2. Add the carrots, chili paste, chopped tomatoes and the rest of the ingredients into the mixture.
3. Cook the dish for ten minutes.
4. Add the ramen into the mixture once the sauce is ready.
5. Mix the ramen well.
6. Cook the dish for five minutes.
7. Add the green onions into the dish.
8. Your dish is ready to be served.

5.14 Japanese Vegan Shōyu Ramen with Potatoes Recipe

Preparation Time: 20 minutes
Cooking Time: 20 minutes
Serving: 4

Ingredients:

- Ramen noodles, two packs
- Chopped potatoes, one cup
- Spicy chili bean sauce, two teaspoon
- Onion, one cup
- Dashi stock, two cups
- Japanese fresh herbs, half teaspoon
- Minced garlic, two tablespoon
- Minced ginger, two tablespoon
- Cilantro, half cup
- Chili oil, two tablespoon
- Shredded nori sheets, half cup
- Sheragi negi, two cups
- Chopped tomatoes, one cup

Instructions:

1. Take a pan.
2. Add in the oil and onions.
3. Cook the onions until they become soft and fragrant.
4. Add in the chopped garlic and ginger.
5. Cook the mixture for a few seconds.
6. Add the spices.
7. Add the sgeragi negi and chopped potatoes into it when the spices are done.
8. Mix the ingredients carefully and cover the pan.
9. Add the rest of the ingredients except the noodles.

10. Let the mixture boil.
11. Add the ramen noodles into the mixture.
12. Add shredded nori sheets on top.
13. Your dish is ready to be served.

5.15 Japanese Ginger Ramen Recipe

Preparation Time: 10 minutes

Cooking Time: 10 minutes

Serving: 4

Ingredients:

- Water, two cups
- Ramen noodles, two pack
- Ginger paste, one tablespoon
- Mix spice, half cup
- Dashi powder, two tablespoon
- Fresh shiso leaves, a quarter cup
- Sesame oil, one tablespoon

Instructions:
1. Take a large pan.
2. Add all the ingredients into the pan.
3. Cook the ingredients for ten minutes.
4. Garnish it with shiso leaves.
5. Your dish is ready to be served.

5.16 Japanese Vegan Ramen Taco Recipe

Preparation Time: 10 minutes

Cooking Time: 10 minutes

Serving: 4

Ingredients:

- Water, two cups
- Ramen noodle plates, two pack
- Mixed vegetables, one cup
- Ginger paste, one tablespoon
- Mix spice, half cup
- Dashi powder, two tablespoon
- Fresh shiso leaves, a quarter cup
- Sesame oil, one tablespoon

Instructions:

1. Take a large pan.
2. Add the vegetables and rest of the filling ingredients into the pan.
3. Cook the ingredients for ten minutes.
4. Switch off the stove.
5. Boil the ramen noodle plates in boiling water for one minute each.
6. Turn them into taco shape.
7. Add the prepared filling mixture into the taco.

8. Garnish the tacos with shiso leaves.
9. Your dish is ready to be served.

5.17 Japanese Vegetarian Spicy Peanut Tempeh Ramen Recipe

Preparation Time: 30 minutes
Cooking Time: 10 minutes
Serving: 4

Ingredients:

- Peanut sauce, one cup
- Sliced green onions, half cup
- Chili paste, one teaspoon
- Mirin paste, one teaspoon
- Cilantro, one cup
- Bamboo shoots, one teaspoon
- Miso paste, one tablespoon
- Soy sauce, one tablespoon
- Cooking oil, two tablespoon
- Chopped garlic, one teaspoon
- Japanese fresh herbs, half teaspoon
- Fresh shiso leaves, two tablespoon
- Fresh cilantro leaves, half cup
- Dried chili flakes, two teaspoon

- Tempeh cubes, one cup
- Ramen, as required

Instructions:
1. Take a large pan.
2. Add the cooking oil and chopped garlic into the pan.
3. Add the tempeh cubes into the pan.
4. Add all the spices into the mixture.
5. Cook the ingredients for five minutes.
6. Add the peanut sauce and ramen into the mixture.
7. Cook all the ingredients well.
8. Cover the pan for five minutes.
9. Garnish the dish with cilantro and green onions.
10. Your dish is ready to be served.

5.18 Japanese Spicy Soy Milk Ramen Recipe

Preparation Time: 30 minutes
Cooking Time: 10 minutes
Serving: 4

Ingredients:

- Soy milk, one cup

- Chili paste, one tablespoon
- Sliced green onions, half cup
- Mirin paste, one teaspoon
- Cilantro, one cup
- Fresh ginger, one teaspoon
- Miso paste, one tablespoon
- Soy sauce, one tablespoon
- Japanese fresh herbs, half teaspoon
- Fresh shiso leaves, two tablespoon
- Fresh cilantro leaves, half cup
- Minced lemon grass, one teaspoon
- Ramen, as required

Instructions:

1. Add all the ingredients of the sauce i.e. miso paste, soy sauce, mirin paste and Japanese fresh herbs into a large pan.
2. Add the soy milk and the rest of the ingredients into the mixture.
3. Cook the dish for ten minutes.
4. Add the ramen into the mixture once the sauce is ready.
5. Mix the ramen well.
6. Cook the dish for five minutes.
7. Add the cilantro into the dish.
8. Your dish is ready to be served.

5.19 Japanese Vegetarian Ginger and Scallion Ramen Recipe

Preparation Time: 10 minutes
Cooking Time: 10 minutes
Serving: 4

Ingredients:

- Water, two cups
- Ramen noodles, two pack
- Ginger slices, half cup
- Mix vegetables, one cup
- Chopped scallions, half cup
- Mix spice, half cup
- Dashi powder, two tablespoon
- Fresh shiso leaves, a quarter cup
- Sesame oil, one tablespoon

Instructions:
1. Take a large pan.
2. Add all the vegetables and oil into the pan.
3. Add the spices and sauces into the pan.
4. Cook the ingredients for five minutes and add the ramen noodles.
5. Cook the ingredients for ten minutes.

6. Garnish it with ginger slices and scallions on top.
7. Your dish is ready to be served.

5.20 Japanese Crispy Sesame Tofu Ramen Recipe

Preparation Time: 20 minutes
Cooking Time: 10 minutes
Serving: 4

Ingredients:

- Sesame seeds, half cup
- Sliced green onions, half cup
- Mirin paste, one teaspoon
- Cilantro, one cup
- Fresh ginger, one teaspoon
- Soy sauce, one tablespoon
- Japanese fresh herbs, half teaspoon
- Fresh shiso leaves, two tablespoon
- Fresh cilantro leaves, half cup
- Minced lemon grass, one teaspoon
- Ramen, as required
- Tofu cubes, one cup
- Corn starch, two teaspoon
- Cooking oil, as required

Instructions:
1. Heat a large pan.
2. Add the cooking oil and let it heat.
3. Mix the tofu cubes, sesame seeds and cornstarch in a bowl.
4. Add the tofu cubes into the heated oil.
5. Cook the tofu well for about five minutes.
6. Dish out the tofu cubes and set aside when done.
7. Add the miso paste and the rest of the ingredients into the mixture.
8. Cook the ingredients for ten minutes.
9. Add the ramen into the mixture once the sauce is ready.
10. Mix the ramen well.
11. Cook the dish for five minutes.
12. Add the crispy sesame tofu on top.
13. Add the cilantro into the dish.
14. Your dish is ready to be served.

Conclusion

Japanese noodle soups aka ramen is one of the easiest comfort food that you can prepare at home. Ramen soups come in different varieties. You can have vegetarian soups as well as non-vegetarian soups. All these soups are healthy and full of taste for ramen lovers around the world.

After reading this book, you will realize that making your favorite Japanese food at home is not difficult at all. In this book, we discussed in detail the history and origin of ramen. The various ingredients used in cooking ramen have also been mentioned in this book. This cookbook includes 70 recipes that contain breakfast, lunch, dinner, and vegetarian recipes. You can easily make these recipes at home without supervision of any kind. So, start cooking today and enjoy cooking your delicious ramen at home.

THAI COOKBOOK

70 Easy Recipes for Traditional Food from Thailand

Maki Blanc

© **Copyright 2021 by Maki Blanc - All rights reserved.**

This document is geared towards providing exact and reliable information in regard to the topic and issue covered. The publication is sold with the idea that the publisher is not required to render accounting, officially permitted, or otherwise, qualified services. If advice is necessary, legal or professional, a practiced individual in the profession should be ordered.

From a Declaration of Principles which was accepted and approved equally by a Committee of the American Bar Association and a Committee of Publishers and Associations.

In no way is it legal to reproduce, duplicate, or transmit any part of this document in either electronic means or in printed format. Recording of this publication is strictly prohibited and any storage of this document is not allowed unless with written permission from the publisher. All rights reserved.

The information provided herein is stated to be truthful and consistent, in that any liability, in terms of inattention or otherwise, by any usage or abuse of any policies, processes, or directions contained within is the solitary and utter responsibility of the recipient reader. Under no circumstances will any legal responsibility or blame be held against the publisher for any reparation, damages, or monetary loss due to the information herein, either directly or indirectly.

Respective authors own all copyrights not held by the publisher.

The information herein is offered for informational purposes solely and is universal as so. The presentation of the information is without contract or any type of guarantee assurance.

The trademarks that are used are without any consent, and the publication of the trademark is without permission or backing by the trademark owner. All trademarks and brands within this book are for clarifying purposes only and are owned by the owners themselves, not affiliated with this document.

Introduction

Food is an indispensable part of our every day schedule. Without the addition of solid, nutritious, and scrumptious food, life can truly transform into a test. Cooking is viewed as a difficult task because of the lack of our cooking abilities or exposure to the authentic recipes of different cuisines.

This book is principally about Thai cuisine. Thai food is the public cooking of Thailand. Thai cooking places accentuation on light meals with amazing aromatic segments and a spicy or zesty edge. Thai cooking is about the shuffling of different components to make an amicable completion i.e. like an unpredictable melodic harmony, it must have a smooth surface, yet it does not make a difference what goes on underneath.

In this cookbook, you will come across the history and origin of Thai food as well as the history of traditional Thai dishes. You are going to get a brief information regarding the evolution of Thai cuisine over the years.

There are various health benefits of having Thai food at home, and you will know all of these benefits when you go through the different properties of spices used in Thai foods. You will get over 70 different breakfast, lunch, dinner, and dessert, and authentic recipes that are only eaten by Thai people. You can easily start cooking at home with the detailed instructions present below each recipe.

Preparing your Thai food at home without the need to order food from some restaurant can become very easy, once you start reading this book. So, why wait for more? Let us dive deep into the world of Thai cuisine.

Chapter 1: Introduction to Thai Food

Thailand is the most hailed country in the whole world for its cuisine. From the southern landmass toward the northern locales, the country offers a diverse blend of an irresistibly delightful food.

The south of Thailand is acclaimed for its blazing curries, profound usage of coconut milk, and astonishing fish plans. The northeastern part is striking for its veggie filled plates of blended greens and flavors, grilled meat, sausages, and tenacious rice. Bangkok, the greatest city, attracts Thais from all over the country to make an endless mix of alluring flavors to taste.

From streak cooked sautés to hand beaten servings of blended greens, you can find the variety of mouthwatering flavors. If you value eating, you will be in a paradise with the combination and variety of food in this cuisine.

1.1 History and Origin of Thai Food

Thai food started with the people who emigrated from the southern Chinese regions many years back to the land of Thailand. There was a great Szechwan impact on Thai cooking. In any case, all through the long haul, various things have affected Thai food.

Previously, Buddhist clerics carried an Indian touch to the food, and southern Muslim states influenced the cooking in the south of Thailand. Much later, Thai food was affected by European cooking after contact with Portuguese clergymen and Dutch merchants. During this Time, there was some effect from the Japanese as well.

Thailand is a significant country with a distinct geography, and all through the long haul, this has provoked the improvement of nearby divergences in its style of food varieties.

1.2 History of Traditional Thai Dishes

In the beginning, Thai food was usually eaten while sitting on mats or covers on the floor. These traditions are still found in the more customary and traditional families. Right now, there are four distinct styles of cooking in Traditional Thai food:

- The focal region of Thailand offers food that is somewhere between the north and south. In any case, fragrant Jasmine rice is liked by numerous individuals in the area.

- Southern Thai cooking is the most standard and traditional style for cooking in Thailand since that is the essential tourist territory of the country. In southern cooking, there is significantly more use of coconut milk in various dishes. Coconut replaces Ghee for fricasseeing, and there is a significant usage of fish in majority of their dishes.

- The cooking in northern Thailand is ordinarily milder than in the rest of the country. Firm rice is liked, usually it is kneaded into little balls with the fingers and this is one of the most traditional dishes of Thailand.

- The food in the north east is affected by Laos. The food is astoundingly spiced, and tenacious glutinous rice is the supported staple for north-eastern dishes. Regardless of the point that there are great deals of meat dishes in this section of Thailand, meat was inadequate in these towns, and the highest of protein were shrimp and freshwater fish.

1.3 Evolution of Thai Food over Time

Customarily, while Thai cooking, you do not have to think much as there are a variety of foods available. Thus, arranging food requires heaps of interest and participation, including the family members to cook it all together. The food explains the Thai life and its traditions, customs, and culture. Thai families are gigantic and well-weave. In cooking, Thai family members help each other as a group. In cooking curries, young people assist with light work like nipping off basil leaves, and adults help in pounding chilies and other flavors.

In the current day, making Thai food is much less difficult as each of the ingredients are expeditiously open in general stores, yet there is an examination that it does not have the standard principles of the past.

1.4 Thai Foods According to Nutrition and Dietetics

Thai food is normally adored in the United States, and this food has some amazing nutritional benefits as well. The traditional eating routine of Thailand features striking vegetables, fish, and meats that are given rice or noodles and arranged with flavors like turmeric, galangal, Thai basil, and lemongrass. Food served at Western Thai eateries shares numerous parts of valid Thai cooking, despite the fact that it has some striking contrasts.

Thai menus in America may have greater fragments, more singed nourishments, and plans that are higher in salt and sugar. Following are the curative advantages of Thai food:

- The most generally utilized veggies in Thai dinners are flavorful, like peppers, tomato, cabbage, broccoli, carrots, and onions. These veggies are stacked with fiber, nutrients, minerals, and an assortment of mixtures that add to great absorption and general wellbeing.

- Several of the most well-known Thai ingredients are nutritious, yet there are other sound parts of Thai food. For one, Thai suppers frequently highlight a decent equilibrium of macronutrients like protein, fats, and carbs.
- Eating dinners which to a great extent involve non-bland veggies and furthermore contain protein and fat can assist you with keeping up stable glucose levels for the whole day. This, thusly, prompts supported energy and may help weight reduction.
- Curries, pan-sears, and soups are made with an assortment of vegetables, incorporate a protein source like tofu, lean meat, or fish, and contain coconut milk, nut sauces, or other good fats.

Thai food is known for joining provincial spices and flavors, vegetables, and lean proteins that add both flavor and nourishments to suppers. Nonetheless, some Westernized Thai dishes are pan fried, served in segments, or contain unreasonable measures of added sugar and salt. To pick a solid Thai feast, decide on a dish that are stacked with plant food varieties, contains a protein source, and highlights an assortment of spices and flavors.

1.5 Key Ingredients Used in Thai Food

A large portion of the ingredients found in Thai food are a clear reflection of the environment warm, fertile land and abundant water.

Recipes contain fish, unusual products of the soil, a few sorts of noodles and sauces. Rice is the mainstay of most meals.

Hot flavoring mixes are utilized to season everything from the day's catch to the easy to make servings of rice or noodles. Following are a portion of the primary ingredients utilized in Thai cooking:

- Cumin: Thai cooks broil fragrant, natural cumin seeds in a dry container to draw out its flavor, and afterward granulate it for use in curry pastes and other zest mixes. Cumin is likewise an essential fixing in many flavor mixes, soups, stews, meat, bean and rice dishes.

- Basil: Basil is utilized both as an enhancing flavor and a topping in Thai cooking. Small bunch of basils are commonly used in soups, curries and sautés.

- Cinnamon: Thai cooks favor Chinese cinnamon, or Cinnamomum cassia, which is better, to some degree spicier, and more uncommon in shading and flavor than Cinnamomum zeylanicum.

- Garlic: Thai cooks use garlic for its health properties, fragrance, and the way that its flavor mixes well with an assortment of different flavors. Garlic is a principle ingredient in the customary Big Four Seasonings Blend, alongside salt, cilantro root, and white peppercorns.

- Cardamom: The fragrant cardamom seedpod is utilized in a couple of Thai dishes of Indian inception, as Mussaman curry. Somewhat lemony, cardamom additionally has a marginally peppery and sweet taste as well as fragrance. Thai cooks frequently consolidate cardamom with other sweet-smelling flavors, similar to cinnamon, nutmeg, and mace.

- Lemongrass: The light, lemony flavor and aroma of lemongrass is an important staple in Thai food. Thai cooks utilize the bulb and base leaves of lemongrass to prepare sauces, soups, pan-sears and curries. It improves meats, poultry, fish, and vegetables, and it is particularly delectable with garlic, chilies and cilantro.

- Turmeric: The robes of Buddhist priests in Thailand are shaded with antiquated yellow color produced using turmeric. Its flavor is sweet, warm, and somewhat peppery. However, it is utilized principally for shading in numerous Thai dishes, including curries, toppings, fish and grain dishes.

- Curry Powders and Pastes: Thais generally mix their own curry powders and pastes by pounding different spices and flavors in a mortar and pestle. Curries are utilized to season coconut milk, serving of mixed greens dressings, noodle sauces, fish and meat dishes, vegetable dishes and soups.

- Chili peppers: Thai food is hot, because of its liberal utilization of new and dried stew peppers. Despite the fact that stew peppers are not local, they are presently fundamental for Thai food.

- Coriander: The strongly fragrant and somewhat interesting kind of coriander seeds is valued in Thai cooking. Thai cooks utilize the root and the leaf of the plant.

- Galangal: A relative of ginger, this light yellow zest has a sharp, lemony, peppery hot taste. It is otherwise called galingale, Java root, or Siamese ginger. Enormous, slim bits of galangal are utilized to season Thai soups, stews and curries; for pastes, it is finely sliced and beat. Ginger might be a replacement for galangal in most Thai plans.

- Mace: It has somewhat nutty, warm taste and found in soups, stuffing, sauces and heated products. It supplements fish, meats, and cheddar, just as certain refreshments.

- Cilantro: Also known as Chinese parsley, Thais utilize this delicate, verdant plant for its unmistakable flavor and natural or amazing fragrance.

- Nutmeg: Thai cooks appreciate the extreme fragrance and sweet, zesty kind of nutmeg in recipes for sweet and appetizing dishes. The chefs utilize a grater to finely powder the nutmeg.

- Cloves: This dim earthy colored, sweet-smelling zest is utilized in the Thai kitchen. Its taste is particular, sharp, and warm or sweet, and you will discover it in both sweet and savory plans.

Thai food will engage any cook who adores the art of seasoning. And while many dishes are very hot, those prepared at home can be adjusted to just the right degree for your own tastes.

Chapter 2: The World of Traditional Thai Breakfast Recipes

Following are some classic traditional Thai breakfast recipes that are rich in healthy nutrients and you can easily make them with the detailed instructions list in each recipe:

2.1 Salapao Recipe

Preparation Time: 30 minutes

Cooking Time: 15 minutes

Serving: 4

Ingredients:

- Sugar, half tablespoon
- Ground pork, half pound
- Soy sauce, one tablespoon
- Finely chopped shallots, one tablespoon
- Chopped garlic, half tablespoon
- Thai pepper powder, half teaspoon

For the dough:

- Vegetable oil, one tablespoon
- Milk, one cup
- Mixed flour, one and a half cup
- Sugar, four tablespoon

Instructions:
1. Take a large bowl.
2. Add the mixed flour and sugar.
3. In a separate bowl, add vegetable oil and the milk.
4. Add the dry ingredients into the wet ingredients.
5. Knead the dough until it turns semi soft.
6. In a pan, add the ground pork.
7. Cook your pork and then add the finely chopped shallots.
8. Cook your pork until the color of the pork changes.
9. Once the color changes, add the soy sauce, sugar, Thai pepper powder and the chopped garlic.
10. Once the pork is done, knead the dough into small round buns.
11. Add the ground pork into the buns and cover the buns all over.
12. Place the buns in the steamer and steam your buns.
13. Steam your buns for ten to fifteen minutes.
14. Your dish is ready to be served.

2.2 Khao Neow Sang Kaya Recipe

Preparation Time: 30 minutes

Cooking Time: 10 minutes

Serving: 4

Ingredients:

- Coconut cream, one cup
- Vanilla extract, one teaspoon
- Eggs, four
- Palm sugar, half cup
- Coconut milk, one cup

Instructions:
1. In a large bowl, add eggs and beat them well.
2. Beat the eggs until it forms a foamy structure.
3. Add the coconut cream and vanilla extract.
4. Beat the mixture and form a fluffy mixture.
5. Add the coconut milk and palm sugar.
6. Mix everything well and form a homogenized mixture.
7. Add the mixture into a greased pan.
8. Add the pan into a steamer.
9. Steam your mixture for ten minutes.
10. Dish out your mixture and cut into pieces.
11. Your dish is ready to be served.

2.3 Khanum Pang (Thai Waffles) Recipe

Preparation Time: 30 minutes

Cooking Time: 10 minutes

Serving: 4

Ingredients:

- Rice flour, one cup
- Eggs, two
- Chopped fresh cilantro, half cup
- Coconut milk, one cup
- Salt to taste
- Shredded coconut, half cup
- Cardamom powder, two tablespoon

Instructions:

1. Heat your waffle maker.
2. Always remember you heat your waffle maker till the point that it starts producing steam.
3. Remove the egg whites in a bowl and beat them to the point that they become fluffy.
4. Beat the egg yolks in a separate bowl.
5. Add in the egg yolks in the egg whites and delicately mix them with a spatula.
6. Combine the eggs and the rest of the ingredients.
7. When your waffle maker is heated adequately, pour in the mixture.

8. Close your waffle maker.
9. Let your waffle cook for five to six minutes approximately.
10. When your waffles are done, dish them out.
11. Add on top of the waffles the chopped cilantro leaves.
12. Your dish is ready to be served.

2.4 Khanom Recipe

Preparation Time: 30 minutes

Cooking Time: 25 minutes

Serving: 4

Ingredients:

- Cornstarch, three tablespoon
- Salt, as required
- Fresh chopped chives, two tablespoon
- Full-fat coconut milk, two cups
- Unsweetened shredded coconut, a quarter cup
- Rice flour, two cups
- Sugar, half cup
- White rice (cooked), three tablespoon
- Canola oil, as required

Instructions:
1. In a large bowl add the coconut milk.
2. With the help of an electrical beater, beat the coconut milk for approximately ten minutes.
3. You will see that after ten minutes, the coconut milk would be fluffy.
4. In a grinder, add the white rice and unsweetened shredded coconut.
5. Grind your ingredients into a fine paste without any granules.
6. Now add this mixture into the beaten coconut milk.
7. Fold your mixture well.
8. Add the rice flour, cornstarch and sugar into the mixture.
9. The mixture will become a little heavier but remember not to beat the mixture, rather fold it so the air spaces are kept intact.
10. Mix all the left ingredients into the coconut milk mixture.
11. In a muffin tray, add your coconut milk mixture.
12. Grease the muffin tray with canola oil.
13. Steam your mixture for approximately ten to fifteen minutes.
14. When your khanom is cooked, dish it out.
15. Your dish is ready to be served.

2.5 Khai Luak (Thai Soft Eggs) Recipe

Preparation Time: 30 minutes
Cooking Time: 10 minutes
Serving: 4

Ingredients:

- Vegetable oil, one and a half tablespoon
- Cooked pork chops, one cup
- Eggs, four
- Sliced scallions, four
- Sliced shallots, two medium sized
- Cooked barley, one cup
- Fresh coriander leaves, half cup
- Fish sauce, one tablespoon
- Lime juice, two tablespoon
- Sliced red chili, one long

Instructions:
1. In a medium bowl, mix together the lime juice, fish sauce, one teaspoon of the chili paste, and the cooked grains.
2. Put the eggs and the excess half teaspoon of chili paste in a little bowl.

3. Beat with a fork to mix everything.
4. In a huge weighty sauté dish, heat half tablespoon of the oil over medium-high warmth.
5. Add the shallots, the white areas of the scallions, and the pork, (if utilizing) and cook, blending infrequently, until the shallots are dim earthy colored and withered.
6. Cook for four more minutes.
7. Add the scallion greens and the leftover half tablespoon of oil and cook briefly.
8. Pour in the egg blend and cook for thirty seconds, at that point turn and mix your eggs.
9. Pour in the mixture of the grain and cook, turning with a spatula, until it is cooked properly.
10. Your dish is ready to be served.

2.6 Khao Rad Gyang (Thai Breakfast Rice and Curry) Recipe

Preparation Time: 30 minutes

Cooking Time: 10 minutes

Serving: 4

Ingredients:

- Thai chilies, two
- Jalapeno, one large
- Sliced green onions, half cup
- White peppercorns, one teaspoon
- Cilantro, one cup

- Fresh ginger, one teaspoon
- Fish sauce, one tablespoon
- Soy sauce, one tablespoon
- Chinese 5 spice, half teaspoon
- Chili garlic sauce, two tablespoon
- Fresh cilantro leaves, half cup
- Thai basil leaves, a quarter cup
- Beef broth, one can
- Minced lemon grass, one teaspoon
- Egg, one large
- Cooked rice, as required

Instructions:
1. Add all the ingredients of the curry into a pan.
2. Add the beef broth and sauces into the mixture.
3. Cook your dish for ten minutes.
4. Add the cooked rice into the mixture once the curry is ready.
5. Mix the rice well and cook it for five minutes.
6. Add the egg into the pan by pushing the rest of the ingredients to a side.
7. Cook the egg and then mix the rest of the ingredients into it.
8. Cook your dish for five more minutes.
9. Add the cilantro into the dish.
10. Mix your rice and then dish it out.

11. Your dish is ready to be served.

2.7 Khao Yum (Thai Breakfast Rice Salad) Recipe

Preparation Time: 10 minutes
Cooking Time: 30 minutes
Serving: 4

Ingredients:

- Water, two tablespoon
- Turmeric powder, one pinch
- Salt to taste
- Garlic cloves, four
- Cooked rice, one cup
- Mix veggies, one cup
- Olive oil

For Thai Dressing:

- Fish sauce, half tablespoon
- Brown sugar, half tablespoon
- Chopped small chili, one
- Water, one tablespoon
- Peanut oil, one teaspoon
- Rice vinegar, half tablespoon
- Sweet chili sauce, half tablespoon

Instructions:

1. Take a large bowl.
2. Add the ingredients for the dressing into the bowl.
3. Mix everything well enough to form a homogeneous mixture.
4. In the next bowl, add the ingredients for the salad.
5. Add the ingredients for the salad into a pan.
6. Cook your ingredients for five to ten minutes.
7. Add the ingredients into a bowl.
8. Add the dressing on top and mix all the ingredients well.
9. Your dish is ready to be served.

2.8 Thai Breakfast Rice and Shrimp Soup Recipe

Preparation Time: 30 minutes

Cooking Time: 10 minutes

Serving: 4

Ingredients:

- White peppercorns, one teaspoon
- Cilantro, one cup
- Shrimps, 150 grams
- Fish sauce, one tablespoon
- Soy sauce, one and a half tablespoon

- Pork stock, three cup
- Jasmine rice, four cups
- Garlic cloves, four

Instructions:
1. Crush the white peppercorns until they turn into powdered form.
2. At that point, add garlic and cilantro and pound until they are crushed.
3. Add portion of this paste to your shrimps and blend well.
4. Sauté the shrimps in a dish with a drop of oil just until it is cooked through.
5. Deglaze the container with some stock and scratch any pieces of spice adhered to the base.
6. Remove from skillet.
7. Bring the stock to a bubble in a pot, add the other portion of the spice paste and stew briefly.
8. Season with fish sauce and soy sauce, at that point taste and add more if you prefer.
9. When prepared to serve, heat the stock to the point of boiling.
10. Add the rice and the shrimp into the stock.
11. Add the soup into a bowl.
12. Garnish it with cilantro leaves.
13. Your dish is ready to be served.

2.9 Thai Styled Traditional Omelet Recipe

Preparation Time: 30 minutes
Cooking Time: 10 minutes
Serving: 4

Ingredients:

- Bean sprouts, one cup
- Fresh coriander leaves, half cup
- Fish sauce, one tablespoon
- Lime juice, two tablespoon
- Sliced red chili, one long
- Green beans, one cup
- Vegetable oil, one and a half tablespoon
- Sliced mushrooms, one cup
- Eggs, eight
- Sliced red capsicum, one large
- Chopped tomatoes, two medium sized

Instructions:
1. Beat the eggs, quarter cup water, lime juice, fish sauce and a large portion of the chili in an enormous container.

2. Heat two teaspoons of oil in a medium non-stick skillet over medium-high warmth.
3. Cook capsicum and mushrooms, mix, for five minutes or until brilliant and delicate.
4. Add the tomatoes.
5. Cook, mixing, for two minutes or until marginally softened.
6. Boil your green beans in water and then drain them.
7. Combine the mushroom blend, sprouts and beans in a bowl.
8. Warm one teaspoon of residual oil in skillet over medium-high heat.
9. Pour quarter of the egg blend into a dish.
10. Cook for thirty seconds or until just set.
11. Slide the omelet onto a plate.
12. Cover your egg to keep it warm.
13. Garnish by sprinkling with coriander and chili.
14. Your dish is ready to be served.

2.10 Thai Breakfast Ginger and Rice Soup Recipe

Preparation Time: 30 minutes

Cooking Time: 10 minutes

Serving: 4

Ingredients:

- White peppercorns, one teaspoon
- Cilantro, one cup
- Ginger paste, two tablespoon
- Fish sauce, one tablespoon
- Soy sauce, one and a half tablespoon
- Pork stock, three cup
- Jasmine rice, four cups
- Garlic cloves, four

Instructions:

1. Crush the white peppercorns until they turn into powdered form.
2. At that point add garlic and cilantro and pound until they are crushed.
3. Add portion of this paste to your ginger paste and blend well.
4. Bring the stock to a bubble in a pot, add the other portion of the spice paste and stew briefly.
5. Season with fish sauce and soy sauce, at that point taste and add more if you prefer.
6. When prepared to serve, heat the stock to the point of boiling.
7. Add the rice and the ginger paste into the stock.
8. Add the soup into a bowl.
9. Garnish it with cilantro leaves.
10. Your dish is ready to be served.

2.11 Spicy Thai Breakfast Noodles Recipe

Preparation Time: 30 minutes
Cooking Time: 10 minutes
Serving: 4

Ingredients:

- Thai chilies, two
- Jalapeno, one large
- Sliced green onions, half cup
- White peppercorns, one teaspoon
- Cilantro, one cup
- Fresh ginger, one teaspoon
- Fish sauce, one tablespoon
- Soy sauce, one tablespoon
- Chinese 5 spice, half teaspoon
- Chili garlic sauce, two tablespoon
- Fresh cilantro leaves, half cup
- Thai basil leaves, a quarter cup
- Beef broth, one can
- Minced lemon grass, one teaspoon
- Egg, one large
- Cooked noodles, as required

Instructions:
1. Add all the ingredients of the sauce into a pan.
2. Add the beef broth and sauces into the mixture.
3. Cook your dish for ten minutes.
4. Add the cooked noodles into the mixture once the sauce is ready.
5. Mix the noodles well and cook it for five minutes.
6. Add the egg into the pan by pushing the rest of the ingredients to a side.
7. Cook the egg and then mix the rest of the ingredients into it.
8. Cook your dish for five more minutes.
9. Add the cilantro into the dish.
10. Mix your noodles and then dish it out.
11. Your dish is ready to be served.

2.12 Thai Fried Eggs Recipe

Preparation Time: 30 minutes
Cooking Time: 10 minutes
Serving: 4

Ingredients:

- Spring onions, four

- Tortilla, as required
- Pepper to taste
- Butter, as required
- Salt to taste
- Baby plum tomatoes, four
- Eggs, four
- Cilantro, half cup

Instructions:
1. Put the butter in a pan.
2. Add the spring onions and chili into the small pan.
3. Cook for a couple of minutes until softened.
4. Whisk the milk and eggs in a bowl.
5. Add the eggs to the pan.
6. Fry your eggs.
7. Add the tomatoes and coriander leaves on top.
8. Once cooked, dish it out.
9. Your dish is ready to be served.

Chapter 3: The World of Traditional Thai Lunch Recipes

Following are some classic traditional Thai lunch recipes that are rich in healthy nutrients and you can easily make them with the detailed instructions list in each recipe:

3.1 Thai Coconut and Noodle Soup Recipe

Preparation Time: 30 minutes

Cooking Time: 10 minutes

Serving: 4

Ingredients:

- Galangal, one can
- Chicken stock, two cups
- Minced garlic, one teaspoon
- Palm sugar, two tablespoon
- Shallot, one
- Kaffir lime leaves, four
- Lime wedges
- Lemon grass, two sticks
- Fish sauce, two tablespoon
- Mushrooms, one cup
- Coconut milk, one cup
- Cilantro, a quarter cup

- Noodles, half pound
- Olive oil, one tablespoon

Instructions:

1. Take a large sauce pan.
2. Add the shallots and olive oil.
3. Cook your shallots and then add the mushrooms.
4. When the mushrooms are cooked then add the galangal, chicken stock, and minced garlic.
5. Add the palm sugar and coconut milk.
6. Cook your ingredients until it starts boiling.
7. Add in the noodles, lemon grass and rest of the ingredients into your soup.
8. Cook your ingredients for ten minutes.
9. When your noodles are cooked dish out your soup.
10. Garnish it with cilantro leaves.
11. Your dish is ready to be served.

3.2 Thai Curry Mud Crab Recipe

Preparation Time: 30 minutes
Cooking Time: 10 minutes
Serving: 4

Ingredients:

- Galangal, one can
- Chicken stock, two cups
- Minced garlic, one teaspoon
- Minced ginger, one teaspoon
- Palm sugar, two tablespoon
- Shallot, one
- Kaffir lime leaves, four
- Lime wedges
- Lemon grass, two sticks
- Fish sauce, two tablespoon
- Mix vegetables, one cup
- Coconut milk, one cup
- Cilantro, a quarter cup
- Crab meat, half pound
- Olive oil, one tablespoon

Instructions:
1. Take a large sauce pan.
2. Add the shallots and olive oil.
3. Cook your shallots and then add the vegetables.
4. When the vegetables are cooked then add the galangal, chicken stock, minced garlic and ginger.
5. Add the palm sugar and coconut milk.
6. Cook your ingredients until it starts boiling.

7. Add in the crab meat, lemon grass and rest of the ingredients into your curry.
8. Cook your ingredients for ten minutes.
9. When your crab meat is cooked dish out your curry.
10. Garnish it with cilantro leaves.
11. Your dish is ready to be served.

3.3 Thai Chicken and Sweet Potato Soup Recipe

Preparation Time: 30 minutes

Cooking Time: 10 minutes

Serving: 4

Ingredients:

- Galangal, one can
- Chicken stock, two cups
- Minced garlic, one teaspoon
- Palm sugar, two tablespoon
- Shallot, one
- Kaffir lime leaves, four
- Lime wedges
- Lemon grass, two sticks
- Fish sauce, two tablespoon
- Sweet potatoes, one cup
- Coconut milk, one cup

- Cilantro, a quarter cup
- Chicken meat, half pound
- Olive oil, one tablespoon

Instructions:

1. Take a large sauce pan.
2. Add the shallots and olive oil.
3. Cook your shallots and then add the chicken meat.
4. When the chicken meat is half cooked, add the galangal, chicken stock, and minced garlic.
5. Add the palm sugar and coconut milk.
6. Cook your ingredients until it starts boiling.
7. Add in the sweet potato, lemon grass and rest of the ingredients into your soup.
8. Cook your ingredients for ten minutes.
9. When your sweet potatoes are cooked dish out your soup.
10. Garnish it with cilantro leaves.
11. Your dish is ready to be served.

3.4 Thai Pork and Peanut Curry Recipe

Preparation Time: 30 minutes
Cooking Time: 10 minutes
Serving: 4

Ingredients:

- Galangal, one can
- Chicken stock, two cups
- Minced garlic, one teaspoon
- Minced ginger, one teaspoon
- Chopped onion, half cup
- Kaffir lime leaves, four
- Minced ginger, half tablespoon
- Lemon grass, two sticks
- Fish sauce, two tablespoon
- Peanuts, one cup
- Coconut milk, one cup
- Cilantro, a quarter cup
- Pork meat, half pound
- Olive oil, one tablespoon

Instructions:

1. Take a large sauce pan.
2. Add the chopped onion and olive oil.
3. Cook your chopped onion and then add the pork meat.
4. When the pork meat is half cooked then add the galangal, chicken stock, minced garlic and ginger.
5. Add the coconut milk.
6. Cook your ingredients until it starts boiling.
7. Add in the peanuts, lemon grass and rest of the ingredients into your curry.
8. Cook your ingredients for ten minutes.
9. When the pork meat is cooked completely, dish out your curry.
10. Garnish it with cilantro leaves.
11. Your dish is ready to be served.

3.5 Thai Beef Stir-Fry Recipe

Preparation Time: 10 minutes
Cooking Time: 20 minutes
Serving: 4

Ingredients:

- Fish sauce, two tablespoon
- Soy sauce, half cup

- Beef pieces, three cups
- Tomatoes, two
- Cilantro, half cup
- Salt and pepper, to taste
- Minced ginger, half tablespoon
- Vegetable oil, two tablespoon
- Thai chili peppers, three
- Toasted nuts, half cup
- Onion, one
- Scallions, half cup
- Minced garlic, one teaspoon

Instructions:
1. In a large sauce pan add the shallots and oil.
2. Cook your shallots and then add the ginger and garlic.
3. Cook your ginger and garlic and then add in the beef pieces.
4. Stir fry your beef pieces well.
5. Add all the spices and the rest of the ingredients into your dish except the toasted nuts.
6. When your beef is cooked then add the toasted nuts.
7. Cook your dish for five minutes.
8. Garnish your dish with cilantro.
9. Your dish is ready to be served.

3.6 Thai Minced Chicken Salad Recipe

Preparation Time: 10 minutes
Cooking Time: 20 minutes
Serving: 4

Ingredients:

- Water, two tablespoon
- Turmeric powder, one pinch
- Salt to taste
- Garlic cloves, four
- Cooked chicken mince, one cup
- Olive oil

For Thai Dressing:

- Fish sauce, half tablespoon
- Brown sugar, half tablespoon
- Chopped small chili, one
- Water, one tablespoon
- Peanut oil, one teaspoon
- Rice vinegar, half tablespoon
- Sweet chili sauce, half tablespoon

Instructions:

1. Take a large bowl.
2. Add the ingredients for the dressing into the bowl.
3. Mix everything well enough to form a consistent mixture.
4. In the next bowl, add the ingredients for the salad.
5. Add the ingredients for the salad into a pan.
6. Cook your ingredients for five to ten minutes.
7. Add the ingredients into a bowl.
8. Add the dressing on top and mix all the ingredients well.
9. Your dish is ready to be served.

3.7 Thai Lemongrass Beef Stew with Noodles Recipe

Preparation Time: 30 minutes

Cooking Time: 10 minutes

Serving: 4

Ingredients:

- Galangal, one can
- Beef stock, two cups
- Minced garlic, one teaspoon
- Palm sugar, two tablespoon
- Shallot, one

- Ginger pieces, a quarter cup
- Beef pieces, half pound
- Kaffir lime leaves, four
- Lemon grass, two sticks
- Fish sauce, two tablespoon
- Mixed vegetables, one cup
- Coconut milk, one cup
- Cilantro, a quarter cup
- Noodles, half pound
- Olive oil, one tablespoon

Instructions:
1. Take a large sauce pan.
2. Add the shallots and olive oil.
3. Cook your shallots and then add the mixed vegetables.
4. When the vegetables are cooked then add the galangal, beef stock, and minced garlic.
5. Add the ginger pieces and coconut milk.
6. Cook your ingredients until it starts boiling.
7. Add in the noodles, lemon grass and rest of the ingredients into your soup.
8. Cook your ingredients for ten minutes.
9. When your noodles are cooked dish out your soup.
10. Garnish it with cilantro leaves.
11. Your dish is ready to be served.

3.8 Thai Butternut Squash Soup Recipe

Preparation Time: 30 minutes
Cooking Time: 10 minutes
Serving: 4

Ingredients:

- Galangal, one can
- vegetables stock, two cups
- Minced garlic, one teaspoon
- Palm sugar, two tablespoon
- Shallot, one
- Ginger pieces, a quarter cup
- Butternut squash, half pound
- Kaffir lime leaves, four
- Lemon grass, two sticks
- Fish sauce, two tablespoon
- Coconut milk, one cup
- Cilantro, a quarter cup
- Noodles, half pound
- Olive oil, one tablespoon

Instructions:

1. Take a large sauce pan.
2. Add the shallots and olive oil.
3. Cook your shallots and then add the butternut squash.
4. When the squash is cooked then add the galangal, vegetable stock, and minced garlic.
5. Add the ginger pieces and coconut milk.
6. Cook your ingredients until it starts boiling.
7. Add in the lemon grass and rest of the ingredients into your soup.
8. Cook your ingredients for ten minutes.
9. Garnish it with cilantro leaves.
10. Your dish is ready to be served.

3.9 Thai Green Chicken Soup Recipe

Preparation Time: 30 minutes

Cooking Time: 10 minutes

Serving: 4

Ingredients:

- Galangal, one can
- Chicken stock, two cups
- Minced garlic, one teaspoon
- Palm sugar, two tablespoon

- Shallot, one
- Kaffir lime leaves, four
- Lime wedges
- Lemon grass, two sticks
- Fish sauce, two tablespoon
- Thai green curry paste, two tablespoon
- Coconut milk, one cup
- Cilantro, a quarter cup
- Chicken meat, half pound
- Olive oil, one tablespoon

Instructions:

1. Take a large sauce pan.
2. Add the shallots and olive oil.
3. Cook your shallots and then add the chicken meat.
4. When the chicken meat is half cooked, add the galangal, green curry paste, chicken stock, and minced garlic.
5. Add the palm sugar and coconut milk.
6. Cook your ingredients until it starts boiling.
7. Add in the lemon grass and rest of the ingredients into your soup.
8. Cook your ingredients for ten minutes.
9. When your chicken meat is cooked completely, dish out your soup.
10. Garnish it with cilantro leaves.

11. Your dish is ready to be served.

3.10 Thai Baked Chicken and Rice Recipe

Preparation Time: 30 minutes
Cooking Time: 25 minutes
Serving: 4

Ingredients:

- Minced ginger, two tablespoon
- Cilantro, half cup
- Olive oil, two tablespoon
- Chopped tomatoes, one cup
- Powdered cumin, one tablespoon
- Salt, to taste
- Black pepper, to taste
- Turmeric powder, one teaspoon
- Fresh Thai herbs, two tablespoon
- Onion, one cup
- Smoked paprika, half teaspoon
- Whole chicken, one pound
- Minced garlic, two tablespoon
- Cooked jasmine rice, as required

Instructions:

1. Take a pan.
2. Add in the oil and onions.
3. Cook the onions until they become soft and fragrant.
4. Add in the chopped garlic and ginger.
5. Cook the mixture and add the tomatoes into it.
6. Add the spices.
7. When the tomatoes are done, add the chicken into it.
8. Mix the chicken so that the tomatoes and spices are coated all over the chicken.
9. Place the chicken on a baking tray and cover your chicken with aluminum foil.
10. Place fresh Thai herbs in the chicken.
11. Bake your chicken for fifteen to twenty minutes.
12. When your chicken is done, dish it out.
13. Sprinkle the cilantro on top of the chicken.
14. Cut your chicken into pieces and place it on the jasmine rice.
15. Your dish is ready to be served.

3.11 Thai Pork Belly with Basil and Tofu Recipe

Preparation Time: 30 minutes

Cooking Time: 10 minutes

Serving: 4

Ingredients:

- Thai chilies, two
- Jalapeno, one large
- Sliced green onions, half cup
- Pork belly pieces, two cups
- Tofu cubes, two cups
- White peppercorns, one teaspoon
- Cilantro, one cup
- Fresh ginger, one teaspoon
- Fish sauce, one tablespoon
- Soy sauce, one tablespoon
- Chinese 5 spice, half teaspoon
- Chili garlic sauce, two tablespoon
- Fresh cilantro leaves, half cup
- Thai basil leaves, a quarter cup
- Chicken broth, one can
- Minced lemon grass, one teaspoon

Instructions:
1. Add all the ingredients of the sauce into a pan.
2. Add the chicken broth and sauces into the mixture.
3. Cook your dish for ten minutes.
4. Add the pork belly pieces and tofu pieces into the mixture once the sauce is ready.

5. Mix the ingredients well and cook it for five minutes.
6. Add the basil leaves and then mix the rest of the ingredients into it.
7. Cook your dish for five more minutes.
8. Add the cilantro into the dish.
9. Your dish is ready to be served.

3.12 Thai Red Meatball Curry Recipe

Preparation Time: 30 minutes
Cooking Time: 10 minutes
Serving: 4

Ingredients:

- Galangal, one can
- Chicken stock, two cups
- Minced garlic, one teaspoon
- Palm sugar, two tablespoon
- Shallot, one
- Kaffir lime leaves, four
- Lime wedges
- Lemon grass, two sticks
- Fish sauce, two tablespoon
- Thai red curry paste, two tablespoon
- Coconut milk, one cup

- Cilantro, a quarter cup
- Frozen meatballs, half pound
- Olive oil, one tablespoon

Instructions:
1. Take a large sauce pan.
2. Add the shallots and olive oil.
3. Cook your shallots and then add the meatballs.
4. When the meatballs are half cooked, add the galangal, red curry paste, chicken stock, and minced garlic.
5. Add the palm sugar and coconut milk.
6. Cook your ingredients until it starts boiling.
7. Add in the lemon grass and rest of the ingredients into the curry.
8. Cook your ingredients for ten minutes.
9. When your curry is cooked dish it out.
10. Garnish it with cilantro leaves.
11. Your dish is ready to be served.

3.13 Thai Sesame Chicken Salad Recipe

Preparation Time: 10 minutes
Cooking Time: 20 minutes
Serving: 4

Ingredients:

- White sesame seeds, half cup
- Black sesame seeds, half cup
- Salt to taste
- Garlic cloves, four
- Cooked chicken meat, one cup
- Olive oil

For Thai Dressing:

- Fish sauce, half tablespoon
- Brown sugar, half tablespoon
- Chopped small chili, one
- Water, one tablespoon
- Peanut oil, one teaspoon
- Rice vinegar, half tablespoon
- Sweet chili sauce, half tablespoon

Instructions:
1. Take a large bowl.
2. Add the ingredients for the dressing into the bowl.
3. Mix everything well enough to form a smooth mixture.
4. In the next bowl, add the ingredients for the salad.
5. Add the ingredients for the salad into a bowl.

6. Add the dressing on top and mix all the ingredients well.
7. Your dish is ready to be served.

3.14 Spicy Thai Prawn Noodles Recipe

Preparation Time: 30 minutes
Cooking Time: 10 minutes
Serving: 4

Ingredients:

- Thai chilies, two
- Jalapeno, one large
- Sliced green onions, half cup
- White peppercorns, one teaspoon
- Cilantro, one cup
- Fresh ginger, one teaspoon
- Fish sauce, one tablespoon
- Soy sauce, one tablespoon
- Chinese 5 spice, half teaspoon
- Chili garlic sauce, two tablespoon
- Fresh cilantro leaves, half cup
- Prawns, two cups
- Fish broth, one can
- Minced lemon grass, one teaspoon
- Cooked noodles, as required

Instructions:

1. Add all the ingredients of the sauce into a pan.
2. Add the fish broth and sauces into the mixture.
3. Cook your dish for ten minutes.
4. Add the cooked noodles into the mixture once the sauce is ready.
5. Mix the noodles well and cook it for five minutes.
6. Add the prawns into the pan by pushing the rest of the ingredients to a side.
7. Cook the prawns and then mix the rest of the ingredients into it.
8. Cook your dish for five more minutes.
9. Add the cilantro into the dish.
10. Mix your noodles and then dish it out.
11. Your dish is ready to be served.

3.15 Thai Red Salmon Curry Recipe

Preparation Time: 30 minutes
Cooking Time: 10 minutes
Serving: 4

Ingredients:

- Galangal, one can
- Fish stock, two cups
- Minced garlic, one teaspoon
- Shallot, one

- Kaffir lime leaves, four
- Lemon grass, two sticks
- Fish sauce, two tablespoon
- Thai red curry paste, two tablespoon
- Cilantro, a quarter cup
- Salmon meat, half pound
- Olive oil, one tablespoon

Instructions:

1. Take a large sauce pan.
2. Add the shallots and olive oil.
3. Cook your shallots and then add the salmon meat.
4. When the salmon meat is half cooked, add the galangal, red curry paste, fish stock, and minced garlic.
5. Cook your ingredients until it starts boiling.
6. Add in the lemon grass and rest of the ingredients into the curry.
7. Cook your ingredients for ten minutes.
8. When your curry is cooked dish it out.
9. Garnish it with cilantro leaves.
10. Your dish is ready to be served.

Chapter 4: The World of Traditional Thai Dinner Recipes

Following are some classic traditional Thai dinner recipes that are rich in healthy nutrients and you can easily make them with the detailed instructions list in each recipe:

4.1 Thai Peanut Chicken and Noodles Recipe

Preparation Time: 30 minutes
Cooking Time: 10 minutes
Serving: 4

Ingredients:

- Galangal, one can
- Chicken stock, two cups
- Minced garlic, one teaspoon
- Minced ginger, one teaspoon
- Chopped onion, half cup
- Noodles, two cups
- Minced ginger, half tablespoon
- Lemon grass, two sticks
- Fish sauce, two tablespoon
- Peanuts, one cup
- Coconut milk, one cup

- Cilantro, a quarter cup
- Chicken meat, half pound
- Olive oil, one tablespoon

Instructions:

1. Take a large sauce pan.
2. Add the chopped onion and olive oil.
3. Cook your chopped onion and then add the chicken meat.
4. When the chicken meat is half cooked then add the galangal, chicken stock, minced garlic and ginger.
5. Add the coconut milk.
6. Cook your ingredients until it starts boiling.
7. Add in the noodles, peanuts, lemon grass and rest of the ingredients into your curry.
8. Cook your ingredients for ten minutes.
9. Garnish it with cilantro leaves.
10. Your dish is ready to be served.

4.2 Thai Red Curry Chicken and Vegetable Recipe

Preparation Time: 30 minutes
Cooking Time: 10 minutes
Serving: 4

Ingredients:

- Galangal, one can
- Chicken stock, two cups
- Minced garlic, one teaspoon
- Shallot, one
- Mix vegetables, one cup
- Lemon grass, two sticks
- Fish sauce, two tablespoon
- Thai red curry paste, two tablespoon
- Cilantro, a quarter cup
- Chicken meat, half pound
- Olive oil, one tablespoon

Instructions:

1. Take a large sauce pan.
2. Add the shallots and olive oil.
3. Cook your shallots and then add the chicken meat and vegetables.
4. When the chicken meat is half cooked, add the galangal, red curry paste, chicken stock, and minced garlic.
5. Cook your ingredients until it starts boiling.
6. Add in the lemon grass and rest of the ingredients into the dish.
7. Cook your ingredients for ten minutes.

8. Garnish it with cilantro leaves.
9. Your dish is ready to be served.

4.3 Thai Noodles with Spicy Peanut Sauce Recipe

Preparation Time: 30 minutes
Cooking Time: 10 minutes
Serving: 4

Ingredients:

- Mixed vegetables, two cups
- Minced garlic, one teaspoon
- Minced ginger, one teaspoon
- Chopped onion, half cup
- Noodles, two cups
- Minced ginger, half tablespoon
- Lemon grass, two sticks
- Fish sauce, two tablespoon
- Spicy peanut sauce, one cup
- Coconut milk, one cup
- Cilantro, a quarter cup
- Olive oil, one tablespoon

Instructions:
1. Take a large sauce pan.
2. Add the chopped onion and olive oil.
3. Cook your chopped onion and then add the vegetables.
4. Add the coconut milk.
5. Cook your ingredients until it starts boiling.
6. Add in the noodles, spicy peanut sauce and the rest of the ingredients.
7. Cook your ingredients for ten minutes.
8. Garnish it with cilantro leaves.
9. Your dish is ready to be served.

4.4 Thai Coconut and Beef Curry Recipe

Preparation Time: 30 minutes

Cooking Time: 10 minutes

Serving: 4

Ingredients:

- Galangal, one can
- Beef stock, two cups
- Minced garlic, one teaspoon
- Crushed ginger, one teaspoon
- Chopped onion, half cup
- Minced ginger, half tablespoon
- Lemon grass, two sticks

- Fish sauce, two tablespoon
- Shredded coconut, one cup
- Coconut milk, one cup
- Cilantro, a quarter cup
- Beef meat, half pound
- Olive oil, one tablespoon

Instructions:

1. Take a large sauce pan.
2. Add the chopped onion and olive oil.
3. Cook your chopped onion and then add the beef meat.
4. When the beef meat is half cooked then add the galangal, beef stock, minced garlic and ginger.
5. Add the coconut milk.
6. Cook your ingredients until it starts boiling.
7. Add in the shredded coconut, lemon grass and rest of the ingredients into your curry.
8. Cook your ingredients for ten minutes.
9. When your beef meat is cooked completely dish out your curry.
10. Garnish it with cilantro leaves.
11. Your dish is ready to be served.

4.5 Thai Coconut and Beef Salad Recipe

Preparation Time: 10 minutes

Cooking Time: 20 minutes

Serving: 4

Ingredients:

- Water, two tablespoon
- Shredded coconut, half cup
- Salt to taste
- Garlic cloves, four
- Cooked beef strips, one cup
- Olive oil

For Thai Dressing:
- Fish sauce, half tablespoon
- Brown sugar, half tablespoon
- Chopped small chili, one
- Water, one tablespoon
- Peanut oil, one teaspoon
- Rice vinegar, half tablespoon
- Sweet chili sauce, half tablespoon

Instructions:
1. Take a large bowl.
2. Add the ingredients for the dressing into the bowl.
3. Mix everything well enough to form a consistent mixture.
4. In the next bowl, add the ingredients for the salad.

5. Add the ingredients for the salad into a bowl and mix properly.
6. Add the dressing on top and mix all the ingredients well.
7. Your dish is ready to be served.

4.6 Thai Green Chicken Thighs Recipe

Preparation Time: 10 minutes
Cooking Time: 40 minutes
Serving: 2

Ingredients:

- Chicken broth, one cup
- Thai green curry paste, one teaspoon
- Onion, one cup
- Lemon juice, half cup
- Chicken thighs, half pound
- Thai spices, half tablespoon
- Water, one cup
- Minced garlic, two tablespoon
- Minced ginger, two tablespoon
- Cilantro, half cup
- Olive oil, two tablespoon

- Chopped tomatoes, one cup

Instructions:
1. Take a pan.
2. Add in the oil and onions.
3. Cook the onions until they become soft and fragrant.
4. Add in the chopped garlic and ginger.
5. Cook the mixture and add the tomatoes into it.
6. Add the spices and chicken thighs.
7. Add in the broth.
8. Mix the ingredients carefully and cover your pan.
9. Add cilantro on top.
10. Your dish is ready to be served.

4.7 Thai Basil Pork Stir-Fry Recipe

Preparation Time: 10 minutes
Cooking Time: 20 minutes
Serving: 4

Ingredients:

- Fish sauce, two tablespoon
- Soy sauce, half cup
- Pork pieces, three cups
- Tomatoes, two

- Cilantro, half cup
- Salt and pepper, to taste
- Minced ginger, half tablespoon
- Vegetable oil, two tablespoon
- Thai chili peppers, three
- Basil leaves, half cup
- Onion, one
- Minced garlic, one teaspoon

Instructions:
1. In a large sauce pan, add the onions and oil.
2. Cook your onions and then add the ginger and garlic.
3. Cook your ginger and garlic and then add in the pork pieces.
4. Stir fry your pork pieces well.
5. Add all the spices and the rest of the ingredients into your dish except the basil leaves.
6. When your pork is cooked then add the basil leaves.
7. Cook your dish for five minutes.
8. Garnish your dish with cilantro.
9. Your dish is ready to be served.

4.8 Thai Green Chicken Curry with Vegetables Recipe

Preparation Time: 30 minutes
Cooking Time: 10 minutes
Serving: 4

Ingredients:

- Galangal, one can
- Chicken stock, two cups
- Minced garlic, one teaspoon
- Shallot, one
- Kaffir lime leaves, four
- Lime wedges
- Lemon grass, two sticks
- Fish sauce, two tablespoon
- Thai green curry paste, two tablespoon
- Mixed vegetables, one cup
- Cilantro, a quarter cup
- Chicken pieces, half pound
- Olive oil, one tablespoon

Instructions:

1. Take a large sauce pan.
2. Add the shallots and olive oil.
3. Cook your shallots and then add the chicken pieces and vegetables.
4. When the chicken pieces are half cooked, add the galangal, green curry paste, chicken stock, and minced garlic.
5. Cook your ingredients until it starts boiling.
6. Add in the lemon grass and rest of the ingredients into your soup.
7. Cook your ingredients for ten minutes.
8. When your chicken pieces are cooked completely dish out your soup.
9. Garnish it with cilantro leaves.
10. Your dish is ready to be served.

4.9 Thai Mussels in Basil Coconut Sauce Recipe

Preparation Time: 30 minutes

Cooking Time: 10 minutes

Serving: 4

Ingredients:

- Galangal, one can
- Fish stock, two cups

- Minced garlic, one teaspoon
- Minced ginger, one teaspoon
- Chopped onion, half cup
- Crushed ginger, half tablespoon
- Basil leaves, a quarter cup
- Fish sauce, two tablespoon
- Shredded coconut, one cup
- Coconut milk, one cup
- Cilantro, a quarter cup
- Mussels, half pound
- Olive oil, one tablespoon

Instructions:
1. Take a large sauce pan.
2. Add the chopped onion and olive oil.
3. Cook your chopped onion and then add the mussels.
4. When the mussels are half cooked then add the galangal, fish stock, minced garlic and ginger.
5. Add the coconut milk.
6. Cook your ingredients until it starts boiling.
7. Add in the shredded coconut, basil leaves and rest of the ingredients into your curry.
8. Cook your ingredients for ten minutes.
9. Garnish it with cilantro leaves.
10. Your dish is ready to be served.

4.10 Thai Pumpkin and Sweet Potato Curry Recipe

Preparation Time: 30 minutes
Cooking Time: 10 minutes
Serving: 4

Ingredients:

- Galangal, one can
- Chicken stock, two cups
- Chopped garlic, one teaspoon
- Palm sugar, two tablespoon
- Shallot, one
- Lemon grass, two sticks
- Fish sauce, two tablespoon
- Sweet potatoes, one cup
- Coconut milk, one cup
- Cilantro, a quarter cup
- Pumpkin pieces, two cups
- Olive oil, one tablespoon

Instructions:
1. Take a large sauce pan.

2. Add the shallots and olive oil.
3. Cook your shallots.
4. When the pumpkin and sweet potatoes is half cooked, add the galangal, chicken stock, and minced garlic.
5. Cook your ingredients until it starts boiling.
6. Add in the lemon grass and rest of the ingredients into your curry.
7. Cook your ingredients for ten minutes.
8. Garnish it with cilantro leaves.
9. Your dish is ready to be served.

4.11 Thai Tofu Fried Rice Recipe

Preparation Time: 30 minutes

Cooking Time: 10 minutes

Serving: 4

Ingredients:

- Tofu cubes, one cup
- Jalapeno, one large
- Sliced green onions, half cup
- White peppercorns, one teaspoon
- Cilantro, one cup
- Fresh ginger, one teaspoon
- Fish sauce, one tablespoon
- Soy sauce, one tablespoon

- Chinese 5 spice, half teaspoon
- Chili garlic sauce, two tablespoon
- Fresh cilantro leaves, half cup
- Thai basil leaves, a quarter cup
- Vegetable broth, one can
- Minced lemon grass, one teaspoon
- Cooked rice, as required

Instructions:

1. Add all the ingredients of the curry into a pan.
2. Add the vegetable broth and sauces into the mixture.
3. Cook your dish for ten minutes.
4. Add the cooked rice into the mixture once the curry is ready.
5. Mix the rice well and cook it for five minutes.
6. Add the tofu pieces into the pan by pushing the rest of the ingredients to a side.
7. Cook the tofu pieces and then mix the rest of the ingredients into it.
8. Cook your dish for five more minutes.
9. Add the cilantro into the dish.
10. Mix your rice and then dish it out.
11. Your dish is ready to be served.

4.12 Thai Chicken Pad Thai Recipe

Preparation Time: 30 minutes
Cooking Time: 10 minutes
Serving: 4

Ingredients:

- Mixed vegetables, two cups
- Sliced green onions, half cup
- White peppercorns, one teaspoon
- Cilantro, one cup
- Fresh ginger, one teaspoon
- Fish sauce, one tablespoon
- Soy sauce, one tablespoon
- Chinese 5 spice, half teaspoon
- Chili garlic sauce, two tablespoon
- Fresh cilantro leaves, half cup
- Thai basil leaves, a quarter cup
- Chicken broth, one can
- Chicken pieces, half pound
- Cooked noodles, as required

Instructions:

1. Add all the ingredients of the sauce into a pan.
2. Add the chicken pieces, vegetables, chicken broth and sauces into the mixture.
3. Cook your dish for ten minutes.
4. Add the cooked noodles into the mixture once the sauce is ready.
5. Mix the noodles well and cook it for five minutes.
6. Add the cilantro into the dish.
7. Mix your noodles and then dish it out.
8. Your dish is ready to be served.

4.13 Thai Sour and Spicy Soup Recipe

Preparation Time: 30 minutes

Cooking Time: 10 minutes

Serving: 4

Ingredients:

- Galangal, one can
- Vegetables stock, two cups
- Minced garlic, one teaspoon
- Palm sugar, two tablespoon
- Shallot, one
- Sweet and sour sauce, half cup
- Ginger pieces, a quarter cup

- Lemon grass, two sticks
- Fish sauce, two tablespoon
- Mixed vegetables, one cup
- Coconut milk, one cup
- Cilantro, a quarter cup
- Olive oil, one tablespoon

Instructions:
1. Take a large sauce pan.
2. Add the shallots and olive oil.
3. Cook your shallots and then add the mixed vegetables.
4. When the vegetables are cooked then add the galangal, vegetable stock, and minced garlic.
5. Add the ginger pieces and coconut milk.
6. Cook your ingredients until it starts boiling.
7. Add in the sweet and sour sauce, lemon grass and rest of the ingredients into your soup.
8. Cook your ingredients for ten minutes.
9. Garnish it with cilantro leaves.
10. Your dish is ready to be served.

4.14 Thai Pumpkin and Coconut Curry Recipe

Preparation Time: 30 minutes
Cooking Time: 10 minutes

Serving: 4

Ingredients:

- Galangal, one can
- Vegetable stock, two cups
- Minced garlic, one teaspoon
- Minced ginger, one teaspoon
- Chopped onion, half cup
- Minced ginger, half tablespoon
- Lemon grass, two sticks
- Fish sauce, two tablespoon
- Shredded coconut, one cup
- Coconut milk, one cup
- Cilantro, a quarter cup
- Pumpkin pieces, half pound
- Olive oil, one tablespoon

Instructions:
1. Take a large sauce pan.
2. Add the chopped onion and olive oil.
3. Cook your chopped onion and then add the pumpkin pieces.
4. When the pumpkin pieces are half cooked then add the galangal, vegetable stock, minced garlic and ginger.

5. Add the coconut milk.
6. Add in the shredded coconut, lemon grass and rest of the ingredients into your curry.
7. Cook your ingredients for ten minutes.
8. Garnish it with cilantro leaves.
9. Your dish is ready to be served.

4.15 Thai Grilled Salmon Recipe

Preparation Time: 30 minutes
Cooking Time: 25 minutes
Serving: 4

Ingredients:

- Minced ginger, two tablespoon
- Cilantro, half cup
- Olive oil, two tablespoon
- Chopped tomatoes, one cup
- Powdered cumin, one tablespoon
- Salt, to taste
- Black pepper, to taste
- Turmeric powder, one teaspoon
- Fresh Thai herbs, two tablespoon
- Onion, one cup
- Salmon filet, one pound

- Minced garlic, two tablespoon

Instructions:

1. Take a pan.
2. Add in the oil and onions.
3. Cook the onions until they become soft and fragrant.
4. Add in the chopped garlic and ginger.
5. Cook the mixture and add the tomatoes into it.
6. Add the spices.
7. Mix the salmon so that the tomatoes and spices are coated all over the salmon.
8. Place fresh Thai herbs on the salmon.
9. Grill your salmon for fifteen to twenty minutes.
10. When your salmon is done, dish it out.
11. Sprinkle the cilantro on top of the salmon.
12. Your dish is ready to be served.

4.16 Thai Red Beef Curry Recipe

Preparation Time: 30 minutes
Cooking Time: 10 minutes
Serving: 4

Ingredients:

- Beef stock, two cups
- Crushed garlic, one teaspoon

- Palm sugar, two tablespoon
- Shallot, one
- Kaffir lime leaves, four
- Lemon grass, two sticks
- Fish sauce, two tablespoon
- Thai red curry paste, two tablespoon
- Cilantro, a quarter cup
- Beef, half pound
- Olive oil, one tablespoon

Instructions:
1. Take a large sauce pan.
2. Add the shallots and olive oil.
3. Cook your shallots and then add the beef meat.
4. When the beef is half cooked, add the red curry paste, beef stock, and minced garlic.
5. Cook your ingredients until it starts boiling.
6. Add in the lemon grass and rest of the ingredients into the curry.
7. Cook your ingredients for ten minutes.
8. When your curry is cooked, dish it out.
9. Garnish it with cilantro leaves.
10. Your dish is ready to be served.

4.17 Thai Coconut Curry Recipe

Preparation Time: 30 minutes
Cooking Time: 10 minutes
Serving: 4

Ingredients:

- Galangal, one can
- Vegetable stock, two cups
- Minced garlic, one teaspoon
- Minced ginger, one teaspoon
- Chopped onion, half cup
- Chopped ginger, half tablespoon
- Lemon grass, two sticks
- Fish sauce, two tablespoon
- Shredded coconut, one cup
- Coconut milk, one cup
- Cilantro, a quarter cup
- Olive oil, one tablespoon

Instructions:
1. Take a large sauce pan.
2. Add the chopped onion and olive oil.
3. Cook your chopped onion.

4. When the onions are cooked then add the galangal, vegetable stock, minced garlic and ginger.
5. Add the coconut milk.
6. Cook your ingredients until it starts boiling.
7. Add in the shredded coconut, lemon grass and rest of the ingredients into your curry.
8. Cook your ingredients for ten minutes.
9. Garnish it with cilantro leaves.
10. Your dish is ready to be served.

4.18 Thai Pumpkin and Vegetable Soup Recipe

Preparation Time: 30 minutes

Cooking Time: 10 minutes

Serving: 4

Ingredients:

- Vegetables stock, two cups
- Minced garlic, one teaspoon
- Galangal, one can
- Shallot, one
- Pumpkin pieces, one cup
- Ginger pieces, a quarter cup
- Lemon grass, two sticks
- Fish sauce, two tablespoon

- Mixed vegetables, one cup
- Coconut milk, one cup
- Cilantro, a quarter cup
- Olive oil, one tablespoon

Instructions:
1. Take a large sauce pan.
2. Add the shallots and olive oil.
3. Cook your shallots and then add the mixed vegetables.
4. When the vegetables are cooked then add the galangal, vegetable stock, and minced garlic.
5. Add the ginger pieces and coconut milk.
6. Cook your ingredients until it starts boiling.
7. Add in the pumpkin, lemon grass and rest of the ingredients into your soup.
8. Cook your ingredients for ten minutes.
9. Garnish it with cilantro leaves.
10. Your dish is ready to be served.

Chapter 5: The World of Traditional Thai Dessert Recipes

Following are some classic traditional Thai dessert recipes that are rich in healthy nutrients and you can easily make them with the detailed instructions list in each recipe:

5.1 Thai Coconut Pudding Recipe

Preparation Time: 10 minutes
Cooking Time: 30 minutes
Serving: 2

Ingredients:
- Coconut Milk, two cups
- White sugar, half cup
- Salt, one teaspoon
- Eggs, two
- Lemon extract, one teaspoon
- Almond extract, one teaspoon
- All-purpose flour, two cups
- Butter, one cup
- Dry yeast, one cup

Instructions:

1. Take a medium bowl and add the butter in it.
2. Add one cup flour and mix well.
3. Then refrigerate it.
4. Take a large bowl and add yeast into it.
5. Add the sugar, the salt and the milk.
6. Mix them well.
7. Mix the warm milk mixture with the flour and the yeast.
8. Add the lemon extract, eggs and almond extract together.
9. Add the baking soda in the mixture.
10. Simmer it for few minutes.
11. Check the thickness of the pudding.
12. Serve warm.

5.2 Thai Fruit Salad Recipe

Preparation Time: 10 minutes
Cooking Time: 30 minutes
Serving: 2

Ingredients:

- Bananas, five or six
- Apples, two or three
- Spring onions, three
- Gem lettuce, separated into leaves

- Lime zest, one
- Chili sauce, one teaspoon
- Fish sauce, one tablespoon
- Rice vinegar, one tablespoon
- Sugar, one tablespoon
- Sesame oil, one tablespoon
- Sesame seeds, one cup

Instructions:

1. Take a large bowl to put all the ingredients into it.
2. First of all, slice the bananas into small pieces so that proper mixing can be done.
3. Then slice the apples in the same way.
4. Put them into the bowl.
5. Add chili sauce and fish sauce into the bowl.
6. Add all spices one by one.
7. Add the rice vinegar in such a way equal distribution can be done.
8. Take the gem lettuce in a separate bowl.
9. Add the lime zest and juice into it.
10. Add the spring onions, sesame seeds and sesame oil into it.
11. Mix all the ingredients so that a good paste is formed
12. Then add it in the first bowl with apples and bananas.
13. You can add sugar as per your requirement.

14. Your salad is ready to be served with chili sauce.

5.3 Thai Mung Bean Pudding Recipe

Preparation Time: 10 minutes
Cooking Time: 15 minutes
Serving: 4

Ingredients:

- Tapioca flour, one cup
- Mung beans, half cup
- Coconut milk, half cup
- White sugar, half cup
- Salt, one teaspoon
- Eggs, two
- Lemon extract, one teaspoon
- Almond extract, one teaspoon
- All-purpose flour, two cups
- Butter, one cup

Instructions:

1. Take a medium bowl and add the mung beans in it.
2. Add one cup tapioca flour and mix well.
3. Then refrigerate it.

4. Take a large bowl and add the coconut milk into it.
5. Add the sugar, salt and milk.
6. Mix them well.
7. Mix the warm milk mixture with the flour and the mung beans.
8. Add the eggs, lemon extract and almond extract together.
9. Add the baking soda in the mixture.
10. Simmer it for few minutes.
11. Check the thickness of the pudding.
12. Your dish is ready to be served.

5.4 Thai Mango Sticky Rice Recipe

Preparation Time: 10 minutes
Cooking Time: 10 minutes
Serving: 4

Ingredients:

- Water, one and a half cup
- Ripe mangoes, two
- Thai sweet rice, one cup
- Coconut milk, one can
- Salt, a quarter teaspoon
- Brown sugar, five tablespoon

Instructions:

1. Add half cup of water, rice, plus half can of the coconut milk, the salt, and one tablespoon of the brown sugar.
2. Stir well.
3. Add coconut milk, salt, and some of the brown sugar to the saucepan.
4. Bring to a gentle boil, and then partially cover with a lid.
5. Reduce heat to medium-low, or just until you get a gentle simmer.
6. Simmer thirty minutes, or until the coconut water has been absorbed by the rice.
7. Turn off the heat but leave the pot on the burner with the lid on it tightly.
8. Allow it to stay for five minutes.
9. To make the sauce, warm the remaining coconut milk over medium-low heat.
10. Add three tablespoons of brown sugar, stirring to dissolve.
11. Prepare the mangoes by cutting them open and slicing each into bite-sized pieces.
12. Scoop some warm rice into each serving bowl, and then drizzle lots of the sweet coconut sauce over the top.
13. Arrange mango slices on the rice and finish with a drizzle of more sauce.
14. Your dish is ready to be served.

5.5 Thai Mango Tapioca Pudding Recipe

Preparation Time: 10 minutes
Cooking Time: 10 minutes
Serving: 4

Ingredients:
- Tapioca flour, one cup
- Mangoes, two
- Coconut milk, half cup
- White sugar, half cup
- Salt, one teaspoon
- Eggs, two
- Lemon extract, one teaspoon
- Almond extract, one teaspoon
- All-purpose flour, two cups
- Butter, one cup

Instructions:
1. Take a medium bowl and add the tapioca flour in it.
2. Add the one cup coconut milk and mix well.
3. Then refrigerate it.

4. Take a large bowl and add the spices into it.
5. Add the sugar, salt and mangoes.
6. Mix them well.
7. Mix the warm milk mixture with the flour and the mangoes.
8. Add the eggs, lemon extract and almond extract together.
9. Add the baking soda in the mixture.
10. Simmer it for few minutes.
11. Check the thickness of the pudding.
12. Your dish is ready to be served.

5.6 Thai Fried Bananas Recipe

Preparation Time: 30 minutes

Cooking Time: 10 minutes

Serving: 4

Ingredients:

- Bananas, five
- Cornstarch, one tablespoon
- Water, two cups
- Coconut milk, one cup
- Rice flour, one cup
- Chinese five spice, as needed
- Cooking oil, as required

Instructions:

1. In a large bowl, add all the ingredients together except the bananas and oil.
2. Mix everything to form a consistent mixture.
3. Dip your bananas into the mixture and then fry them in the cooking oil.
4. Fry your bananas until they turn golden brown.
5. Dish out and drizzle maple syrup if you want on top.
6. Your dish is ready to be served.

5.7 Thai Steamed Banana Cake Recipe

Preparation Time: 10 minutes
Cooking Time: 20 minutes
Serving: 4

Ingredients:

- Bananas, five
- Salt, two tablespoon
- White sugar, two cups
- Cornstarch, one tablespoon
- Water, two cups
- Coconut milk, one cup
- Rice flour, one cup
- Pandan essence, as needed

- Raspberries, aa required

Instructions:
1. Take bananas and peel them.
2. Then steam them properly.
3. Take water in a pot and heat it.
4. Take a large bowl and add the sweet rice into it.
5. Cook the rice and add some of sugar into it for taste.
6. Take another bowl and add coconut milk into it.
7. Mix the palm sugar into the coconut milk.
8. Then mix the rice cooked and coconut milk together.
9. Take them into a large bowl after mixing.
10. Add steamed bananas and raspberries into it.
11. Mix them well and then bake your cake.
12. Your cake is ready to be served.

5.8 Thai Tea Cake Recipe

Preparation Time: 10 minutes
Cooking Time: 40 minutes
Serving: 2

Ingredients:

- Tea, one cup
- Salt, two tablespoon
- White sugar, two cups
- Cornstarch, one tablespoon
- Water, two cups
- Coconut milk, one cup
- Rice flour, one cup
- Pandan essence, as needed
- Raspberries, as required

Instructions:
1. Take one cup of tea.
2. Take water in a pot and heat it.
3. Take a large bowl and add the sweet rice into it.
4. Cook the rice and add some of the sugar into it for taste.
5. Take another bowl and add coconut milk into it.
6. Mix the palm sugar into the coconut milk.
7. Then mix the rice cooked and coconut milk together.
8. Take them into a large bowl after mixing.
9. Mix them well and then bake your cake.
10. Your cake is ready to be served.

5.9 Thai Banana Spring Rolls Recipe

Preparation Time: 10 minutes
Cooking Time: 10 minutes
Serving: 2

Ingredients:

- Chopped bananas, five
- Shredded coconut, half cup
- Wonton wraps, as required
- Chinese five spice, as needed
- Cooking oil, as required

Instructions:
1. In a large bowl, mix all the ingredients together.
2. Add the mixture into the wonton wrappers.
3. Wrap your rolls.
4. Fry your rolls until they turn golden brown.
5. Dish out and drizzle any sauce if you want on top.
6. Your dish is ready to be served.

5.10 Thai Mango Cake Recipe

Preparation Time: 30 minutes

Cooking Time: 10 minutes
Serving: 4

Ingredients:

- Mangoes, three
- Salt, two tablespoon
- White sugar, two cups
- Cornstarch, one tablespoon
- Water, two cups
- Coconut milk, one cup
- Rice flour, one cup
- Raspberries, aa required

Instructions:
1. Take the mangoes into a bowl.
2. Slice them into small pieces.
3. Add salt to it for taste as required.
4. Take water in a pot and heat it.
5. Take a large bowl and add the sweet rice into it.
6. Cook the rice and add some of the sugar into it for taste.
7. Take another bowl and add coconut milk into it.
8. Mix the palm sugar into the coconut milk.
9. Then mix the sliced mangoes and coconut milk together.

10. Take them into a large bowl after mixing.
11. Add the coconut juice and raspberries into it.
12. Mix them well.
13. Then bake them for fifteen minutes.
14. After cooking, you can refrigerate the cake.
15. Your cake is ready to be served.

5.11 Thai Coconut Cake Recipe

Preparation Time: 10 minutes
Cooking Time: 10 minutes
Serving: 4

Ingredients:

- Coconut, two
- Salt, two tablespoon
- White sugar, two cups
- Cornstarch, one tablespoon
- Water, two cups
- Coconut milk, one cup
- Rice flour, one cup
- Raspberries, aa required

Instructions:
1. Take the coconut juice into a bowl.
2. Add salt to it for taste as required.
3. Take water in a pot and heat it.
4. Take a large bowl and add the sweet rice into it.
5. Cook the rice and add some of sugar into it for taste.

6. Take another bowl and add coconut milk into it.
7. Mix the palm sugar into the coconut milk.
8. Then mix the rice cooked and coconut milk together.
9. Take them into a large bowl after mixing.
10. Add the coconut juice and raspberries into it.
11. Mix them well.
12. Then bake them for fifteen minutes.
13. After cooking you can refrigerate the cake.
14. Your cake is ready to be served.

5.12 Thai Mango Ice Cream Recipe

Preparation Time: 10 minutes
Cooking Time: 15 minutes
Serving: 2

- Mangoes, two
- Coconut milk, half cup
- White sugar, half cup
- Salt, one teaspoon
- Eggs, two
- Lemon extract, one teaspoon
- Almond extract, one teaspoon
- All-purpose flour, two cups

- Butter, one cup

Instructions:
1. Slice the mangoes into small pieces.
2. Take a medium bowl and add the tapioca flour in it.
3. Add one cup of coconut milk and mix well.
4. Then refrigerate it.
5. Take a large bowl and add the spices into it.
6. Add the sugar, the salt and the spices.
7. Mix them well.
8. Mix the warm milk mixture with the flour and the sliced mangoes.
9. Add the eggs, the lemon extract and the almond extract together.
10. Add the baking soda in the mixture.
11. Simmer it for few minutes.
12. Check the thickness of the ice cream.
13. Refrigerate it.
14. Your dish is ready to be served.

5.13 Thai Sticky Black Rice Pudding Recipe

Preparation Time: 15 minutes

Cooking Time: 25 minutes

Serving: 3

Ingredients:

- Black rice, two cups
- Chinese sweet spices, to taste
- Coconut milk, half cup
- White sugar, half cup
- Salt, one teaspoon
- Eggs, two
- Lemon extract, one teaspoon
- Almond extract, one teaspoon
- All-purpose flour, two cups
- Butter, one cup

Instructions:
1. Cook the black rice in the rice cooking pan.
2. Take a medium bowl and add the tapioca flour in it.
3. Add one cup of coconut milk and mix well.
4. Then refrigerate it.
5. Take a large bowl and add the spices into it.
6. Add the sugar, the salt and the spices.
7. Mix them well.
8. Mix the warm milk mixture with the flour and the cooked rice.
9. Add the eggs, lemon extract and almond extract together.

10. Add the baking soda in the mixture.
11. Simmer it for few minutes.
12. Your dish is ready to be served.

5.14 Thai Egg and Coconut Custard Recipe

Preparation Time: 30 minutes
Cooking Time: 10 minutes
Serving: 4

Ingredients:
- Eggs, two
- Coconut, two
- Chinese sweet spices, to taste
- Coconut milk, half cup
- White sugar, half cup
- Salt, one teaspoon
- Lemon extract, one teaspoon
- Almond extract, one teaspoon
- All-purpose flour, two cups
- Butter, one cup

Instructions:
1. Take a medium bowl and add the eggs and the tapioca flour in it.
2. Add one cup of coconut milk and mix well.

3. Then refrigerate it.
4. Take a large bowl and add the spices into it.
5. Add the sugar, the salt and the beaten eggs.
6. Mix them well.
7. Mix the warm milk mixture with the flour and coconut.
8. Add the eggs, lemon extract and almond extract together.
9. Add the baking soda in the mixture.
10. Simmer it for few minutes.
11. Check the thickness of the custard.
12. Your dish is ready to be served.

5.15 Thai Sweet Corn Pudding Recipe

Preparation Time: 10 minutes

Cooking Time: 30 minutes

Serving: 4

Ingredients:

- Butter, one cup
- Sweet corn, one cup
- Eggs, two
- Cherries, two
- All-purpose flour, two cups
- Water, as required

- Baking soda, one tablespoon
- Salt, a pinch
- Walnuts, one cup

Instructions:
1. Take a large bowl and clean it well.
2. Add the sweet corn and the baking soda.
3. Add the salt and the cream.
4. Mix all the ingredients well.
5. Add beaten eggs into the mixture.
6. Pour into the dish and spread evenly.
7. Take a small bowl and add the sugar and the butter.
8. Mix them until it becomes smooth.
9. Add the mixture into flour and mix well.
10. Simmer it for about twenty-five minutes
11. Your dish is ready to be served.

Chapter 6: The World of Traditional Thai Recipes Eaten Only by Thai People

Following are some classic traditional Thai recipes eaten only by Thai people that are rich in healthy nutrients and you can easily make them with the detailed instructions list given in each recipe:

6.1 Patonga (Thai Breakfast Donut) Recipe

Preparation Time: 15 minutes

Cooking Time: 30 minutes

Serving: 3

Ingredients:

- All-purpose flour, one cup
- Baking soda, one cup
- Sugar, two tablespoon
- Water, half cup
- Vegetable oil, two cups
- Milk, two cups
- Walnuts, one cup
- Eggs, four
- Cherries, one cup
- Butter as needed

Instructions:

1. Take a large bowl and clean it well.
2. Add the sugar and the baking soda.
3. Add the salt and the cream.
4. Mix all the ingredients well.
5. Add beaten eggs into the mixture.
6. Pour into the dish and spread evenly.
7. Take a small bowl and add the sugar and the butter.
8. Mix them until become smooth.
9. Add the mixture into flour and mix well.
10. Bake it for about twenty-five minutes.
11. Your dish is ready to be served.

6.2 Khanom Kharuk (Thai Mini Pancakes) Recipe

Preparation Time: 30 minutes
Cooking Time: 50 minutes
Serving: 5

Ingredients:

- Blackberry jam, one cup
- Butter, one cup
- Eggs, two
- Cherries, two

- All-purpose flour, two cups
- Water, as required
- Baking soda, one tablespoon
- Salt, a pinch
- Walnuts, one cup

Instructions:
1. Take a large bowl and clean it well.
2. Add the sugar and the baking soda.
3. Add the salt and the cream.
4. Mix all the ingredients well.
5. Add beaten eggs into the mixture.
6. Add blackberry jam into it.
7. Pour into the dish and spread evenly.
8. Take a small bowl and add the sugar and the butter.
9. Mix them until the mixture becomes smooth.
10. Add the mixture into flour and mix well.
11. Bake it for about thirty-five minutes.
12. Your dish is ready to be served.

6.3 Jauk (The Rice Porridge) Recipe

Preparation Time: 20 minutes
Cooking Time: 20 minutes
Serving: 2

Ingredients:

- Fish sauce, three teaspoon
- Brown cooked rice, two cups
- Ground pork, one cup
- Cilantro, one tablespoon
- Black pepper, to taste
- Chicken broth, four cups
- Egg white, half cup
- Galangal, one slice
- Ginger, two tablespoon
- Palm sugar, one tablespoon
- Lime juice, one tablespoon
- Alfa one rice bran oil, teaspoon
- Coconut milk, one cup
- Bean sprouts, one cup
- Fried shallots, to serve
- Red chili, to serve

Instructions:
1. Cook the rice in rice cooker.
2. Then refrigerate it.
3. Prepare meat balls by mixing all the ingredients one by one
4. Cook it for one minute with continuous stirring.

5. Add the coconut milk into the mixture.
6. Boil the coconut milk along with mixture.
7. Continue boiling for five minutes until water reduces to minimum level.
8. Add the egg whites and mix well.
9. Then take the chicken broth in a separate large pot.
10. Add the lemon grass and galangal in it.
11. Simmer it for five minutes.
12. Then add them in already cooked brown rice.
13. Adjust taste by adding pepper and salt.
14. Your soup is ready to be served.
15. Serve it with chilies and soy sauce.

6.4 Khao Tom (The Rice Porridge Soup) Recipe

Preparation Time: 10 minutes
Cooking Time: 25 minutes
Serving: 3

> **Ingredients:**
>
> - Fish sauce, three teaspoon
> - Brown cooked rice, two cups
> - Ground pork, one cup

- Cilantro, one tablespoon
- Black pepper, to taste
- Chicken broth, four cups
- Egg white, half cup
- Galangal, one slice
- Ginger, two tablespoon
- Palm sugar, one tablespoon
- Lime juice, one tablespoon
- Alfa one rice bran oil, teaspoon
- Coconut milk, one cup
- Bean sprouts, one cup
- Fried shallots, to serve
- Red chili, to serve

Instructions:
1. Cook the rice in rice cooker.
2. Then refrigerate it.
3. Prepare meat balls by mixing all the ingredients one by one
4. Cook it for one minute with continuous stirring.
5. Add the coconut milk into the mixture.
6. Boil the coconut milk along with mixture.
7. Continue boiling for five minutes until water reduces to minimum level.
8. Add the egg white and mix well.
9. Then take the chicken broth in separate large pot.

10. Add the lemon grass and galangal in it.
11. Simmer it for five minutes.
12. Then add them in already cooked brown rice.
13. Adjust taste by adding pepper and salt.
14. Your soup is ready to be served.
15. Serve it with chilies and soy sauce.

6.5 Dim Sum (Thai Steamed Buns) Recipe

Preparation Time: 50 minutes
Cooking Time: 30 minutes
Serving: 4

Ingredients:

- Ground pork, half pound
- Thin soy sauce, one tablespoon
- Thai pepper powder, half tablespoon
- Sugar, one tablespoon
- Garlic powder, one tablespoon
- Fresh shallot, half tablespoon
- Milk, one cup
- Vegetable oil, one tablespoon
- All-purpose flour, one cup
- Whole wheat flour, half cup

- Salt, to taste
- Water, to kneed
- Cucumber, one
- Yeast, one cup

Instructions:

1. Take a bowl and add the flour into it.
2. Then add the yeast and sugar into it.
3. Add lukewarm water in it.
4. Set aside for half an hour.
5. In another bowl, take the whole wheat flour.
6. Add the yeast dough in it.
7. Then add the salt and some water in it.
8. Then combine the ingredients to form a soft dough.
9. Knead it for ten minutes.
10. Meanwhile, chop all the vegetables.
11. Mix them with soy sauce, chili vinegar, sugar and salt.
12. Make round forms of dough with the help of the oil.
13. Then bake your buns for ten minutes.
14. Once the buns are steamed, take them out.
15. You can serve Thai buns with salad.

6.6 Thai Sweet Rice Cakes Recipe

Preparation Time: 2 minutes
Cooking Time: 25 minutes
Serving: 2

Ingredients:

- Thai sweet rice, two cups
- Salt, two tablespoon
- White sugar, two cups
- Cornstarch, one tablespoon
- Water, two cups
- Coconut milk, one cup
- Rice flour, one cup
- Pandan essence, as needed
- Raspberries, aa required

Instructions:
1. Take a blender and blend the pandan leaves.
2. Then add the paste type material into a bowl.
3. Press the paste so that all juice comes out.
4. Take the juice and discard the solids.
5. Take water in a pot and heat it.
6. Take a large bowl and add the sweet rice into it.

7. Cook the rice and add some of the sugar into it for taste.
8. Take another bowl and add coconut milk into it.
9. Mix the palm sugar into the coconut milk.
10. Then mix the cooked rice and coconut milk together.
11. Take them into a large bowl after mixing.
12. Add pandan juice and raspberries into it.
13. Mix them well.
14. Then bake them well.
15. After cooking you can refrigerate the cake.
16. Your cake is ready to be served.

6.7 Thai Steamed Pandan Cakes Recipe

Preparation Time: 15 minutes
Cooking Time: 35 minutes
Serving: 2

Ingredients:

- Pandan leaves, one bunch
- Tapioca starch, one cup
- Arrowroot starch, one cup
- Water, two cups
- Coconut milk, one cup

- Rice flour, one cup
- Jasmine tea, one cup

Instructions:
1. Take a blender and blend the pandan leaves.
2. Then add the paste type material into a bowl.
3. Press the paste so that all juice comes out.
4. Take the juice and discard the solids.
5. Take water in a pot and heat it.
6. Take a large bowl and add rice flour into it.
7. Then whisk it with tapioca starch and arrowroot starch.
8. Take another bowl and add coconut milk into it.
9. Mix the palm sugar into the coconut milk.
10. Then mix the rice flour and coconut milk together.
11. Take them into a large bowl after mixing.
12. Add pandan juice and jasmine tea into it.
13. Mix them well and cook them efficiently.
14. After cooking you can refrigerate the whole food.
15. Your cake is ready to be served.

6.8 Thai Carrot and Radish Salad Recipe

Preparation Time: 5 minutes
Cooking Time: 5 minutes
Serving: 3

Ingredients:

- Carrots, two
- Radishes, ten
- Spring onions, three
- Gem lettuce, separated into leaves
- Lime zest, one
- Chili sauce, one teaspoon
- Fish sauce, one tablespoon
- Rice vinegar, one tablespoon
- Sugar, one tablespoon
- Sesame oil, one tablespoon
- Sesame seeds, one cup

Instructions:
1. Take a large bowl to put all the ingredients into it.
2. First of all, slice the carrots into small pieces so that proper mixing can be done.

3. Then slice the radish in the same way.
4. Put them into the bowl.
5. Add chili sauce and fish sauce into the bowl.
6. Add all spices one by one.
7. Add the rice vinegar in such a way that equal distribution can be done.
8. Take the gem lettuce in a separate bowl.
9. Add the lime zest and juice into it.
10. Add the spring onions, sesame seeds and sesame oil into it.
11. Mix all the ingredients so that a good paste is formed
12. Then add it in the first bowl with carrots and radishes.
13. You can add sugar as per your requirement.
14. Your salad is ready to be served with chili sauce.

6.9 Thai Fish Broth with Vegetables Recipe

Preparation Time: 10 minutes

Cooking Time: 25 minutes

Serving: 4

Ingredients:
- Brown rice noodles, one cup
- Chicken, two cups

- Red curry paste, one teaspoon
- Fish sauce, one tablespoon
- White fish, one bowl
- Red chili, to serve
- Prawns, one cup
- Fried shallots, to serve
- Salt, to taste
- Pepper, to taste
- Lime leaves, one cup

Instructions:
1. Take a large saucepan and add oil in it.
2. Heat it over medium high heat.
3. Add the brown rice noodles into it.
4. Cook it for one minute with the continuous stirring.
5. Add the chicken into the mixture.
6. Boil the chicken and curry paste along with mixture.
7. Continue boiling for five minutes until water reduces to minimum level.
8. Add the lime leaves in a separate bowl.
9. And cover it with the boiling water for five minutes.
10. Add fish into the mixture and boil until the meat becomes soft and tender.

11. Add the fish sauce, lime juice and peas into the mixture.
12. Add the prawns to the mixture in the end having all the ingredients.
13. Cook for five minutes so that color and texture of the fish become suitable.
14. Your dish is ready to be served with the sauces and spices you want.

6.10 Thai Prawn and Coconut Soup Recipe

Preparation Time: 10 minutes
Cooking Time: 25 minutes
Serving: 2

Ingredients:

- sauce, three teaspoon
- Palm sugar, one tablespoon
- Lime juice, one tablespoon
- Peas, trimmed, one cup
- Peeled prawns, two cups
- Alfa one rice bran oil, teaspoon
- Coconut milk, one cup
- Bean sprouts, one cup
- Fried shallots, to serve

- Red chili, to serve
- Red curry paste, half cup
- Noodles, one packet

Instructions:
1. Take a large saucepan and add oil in it.
2. Heat it over medium high heat.
3. Add curry paste into it.
4. Cook it for one minute with continuous stirring.
5. Add the coconut milk into the mixture.
6. Boil the coconut milk along with mixture.
7. Continue boiling for five minutes until water reduces to minimum level.
8. Add the noodles in a separate bowl.
9. Cover it with the boiling water for five minutes.
10. Then remove the noodles with the help of fork and drain it.
11. Add the fish sauce, lime juice and peas into the mixture.
12. Add the prawns to the soup.
13. Cook for five minutes.
14. Your soup is ready to be served.

Conclusion

While living a busy life, food becomes the one of the source of happiness for individuals in the 21st century. Different cuisines are available in the world and each of them being totally different from the other, adds delight to the people's lives. Thai cuisine covers dishes from Thailand and Thai foods which are extremely popular in the whole world.

In this book, we have discussed different aspects of Thai cuisine and not only the recipes. We discussed in detail the history and origin of Thai foods. The various spices used in Thai cooking have enormous amount of amazing properties that has such positive and healthy impact on our overall health. This cookbook includes 70 recipes that consist of breakfast, lunch, dinner, dessert, and the recipes that are only eaten by Thai people. You can easily make these recipes at home without supervision of any kind. So start cooking today and enjoy the Thai cuisine more than ever.

Printed in Great Britain
by Amazon